Understanding Learning Disabilities:

A Parent Guide and Workbook

Understanding Learning Disabilities: A Parent Guide and Workbook was developed and written by members of the Learning Disabilities Council as a resource for parents and others concerned about children with learning disabilities. At the time of its development, considerable care and effort were exercised in gathering and verifying information in the Guide. However, neither the Learning Disabilities Council, the National Center for Learning Disabilities nor the publisher is responsible for changes, errors or omissions. Furthermore, neither the Learning Disabilities Council nor the National Center For Learning Disabilities endorses individual consultants, schools, groups or organizations. Neither do they endorse or recommend any specific treatments, therapies, approaches, or techniques. We welcome the input and comments of those utilizing the Guide.

Understanding Learning Disabilities:
A Parent Guide and Workbook

Table of Contents

Dedication

This book is dedicated to all individuals with learning disabilities and their families, in hopes that it will make each day a little better.

Foreword

My heart goes out to all children with learning disabilities and their families. Whether it is a young child, an adolescent or an adult, the pain is the same and it is shared by all. I have a daughter with learning disabilities, and I can certainly empathize with the constant struggles you and your children face. I hope you realize that your child's learning disability is a disability filled with hope. There **are** ways you, and others, can help your child learn and reach his or her true potential. It takes commitment and resources to get that help to the people who need it.

That commitment is never more evident than in groups like The Learning Disabilities Council and the National Center for Learning Disabilities (NCLD). NCLD was founded nearly 15 years ago by Mrs. Carrie (Pete) Rozelle. As the mother of learning disabled sons, Mrs. Rozelle found no help when she needed it most. She established NCLD, to help other parents find the resources for their children, hoping that no other parent would have to go through what she had.

I have now taken the role of Chairman of NCLD for the same reasons. When I first found out my daughter had learning disabilities, my instinct was to do everything humanly possible to help her. Much to my shock and dismay, I learned there was little help available. I felt alone and helpless. At that time, I wondered if other families were going through the same frustration and disappointment. I now realize they were ... and are! We've come a long way since then, but there is still a great deal more that can be done.

That is why I applaud *Understanding Learning Disabilities: A Parent Guide and Workbook*, and all the volunteers and professionals that pulled together to produce it. This workbook captures so many valuable suggestions and guidelines for you as a parent, a teacher, professional, or advocate ... for practically anyone who comes in contact with an individual with learning disabilities.

I first became aware of this workbook through an initiative NCLD started in 1990. We recognized there were many helpful programs and products already in existence for the learning disabled, but so often the resources needed to disseminate and replicate them widely were not available. NCLD selected The Learning Disability Council's workbook as one of the first recipients of our National Replication Award. It is with great pleasure that we are collaborating with such a fine group as The Learning Disabilities Council, in helping this workbook reach a national audience.

Please remember—although frustration and disappointment may continue to arise, there **is great HOPE** for our children. What they need is your love, support, and understanding. Let us all work together to let NO child slip through the cracks, because no one cared enough!

With love and best wishes for children and adults with learning disabilities,

Anne Ford Scarborough
Chairman, National Center for Learning Disabilities (NCLD)

June 5, 1991

Acknowledgements

The publication by the Learning Disabilities Council of *Understanding Learning Disabilities: A Parent Guide and Workbook* has come about through the joint efforts of many people and organizations.

The first edition of the book, published in 1989, was made possible through the generous financial support provided by the Memorial Foundation for Children, Crestar Bank, CSX Corporation and Cadmus Communications.

Initially conceived as a "local" project, the guide was written entirely by volunteer members of the Council, both parents and professionals. After numerous revisions, the book was reviewed by members of the community—parents of learning disabled youngsters, educators, attorneys, advocates, social workers and psychologists. The following individuals were instrumental in bringing the first edition to print:

Writing Committee:
    Elaine S. Ackman
    Robin S. Barton
    Missy Ritsch Chase
    Gweniviere L.C. Hancock
    Ruth Harris
    Inge Horowitz
    Betty Randle
    Jody L. Sands
    Martha C. Yeatts

Editors: Jeanette B. Pollard (resigned September, 1988)
           Mary Louise Trusdell
           Linda S. Williams

Review Committee:
    Maria W. Butler
    Nancy St.C. Finch
    Willie H. Gillenwater
    Robin L. Hawks
    Dorothy Carson-Jones
    Lori Bell Mick
    Jane T. Nott
    Susan B. Spielberg
    Shirley L. Torstrick
    Stan C. Trent

Executive Committee of the Learning Disabilities Council:
    Elaine S. Ackman
    Missy Ritsch Chase
    Patricia W. DeOrio
    Sally C. Elliott, President (1988–1989)
    Harley A. Tomey, President (1987–1988)
    Jack F. Torza
    Mary Louise Trusdell

    Linda S. Williams, Executive Director
    Peter W.D. Wright
    Martha C. Yeatts

The enthusiastic response to the book from parents across the country has prompted this second edition. The Learning Disabilities Council is most grateful to the National Center for Learning Disabilities (NCLD). The very generous grant provided by NCLD has enabled the Council to update and reprint the book and bring it to the attention of parents throughout the United States. In addition to providing this financial undergirding, NCLD's commitment and belief in the project from the outset have been critical. The Council has especially appreciated the encouragement provided by NCLD staff member Rose Crawford. Without the total support of NCLD, this publication might never have become a reality.

The administration of this grant project has been overseen by the following members of the LD Council Advisory Committee:
    Maria C. Butler
    Missy Ritsch Chase
    Carol Harris, President
    Jack F. Torza
    Linda S. Williams, Executive Director

The revision and production of this second edition have been under the supervision of Linda S. Williams, Executive Director of the Learning Disabilities Council. Portions of the book have been re-written to make it applicable to parents across the country. Peter W.D. Wright served as legal consultant in this regard.

The Council would also like to acknowledge the assistance provided by the staff at Amann & Associates Public Relations, Inc., most particularly Laura B. O'Brien, for her enthusiastic, "can-do" attitude.

How to Use This Book

The Purpose of This Guide

This book is expressly intended for parents of suspected or identified learning disabled (LD) children, adolescents, and young adults. In addition, it is intended to be a resource for teachers and professionals who come into contact with individuals with learning disabilities.

Since no one book can hope to answer all the questions which a parent may have, this guide has been designed to be a working tool, comprehensive in its own right, but one that can also grow as parents gather information. When used as suggested, the book will be a …

- source of information
- "how to" guidebook
- workbook
- reference
- filing system

Materials Needed

The following materials are needed to make this book a working tool:

- a large three-ring binder (the bigger the better; oversize binders are generally available at stationery or office supply stores)
- notebook tab dividers (20)
- pack of loose leaf paper
- notebook hole reinforcers
- paper hole puncher
- "post it" sticky note pad
- three hole punched pocket folders (3–5)

We suggest gathering all needed supplies as soon as possible. One quickly discovers upon reading below and throughout the book that organization **now** will save time and many headaches later.

Reading the Guide

We recommend briefly skimming the Table of Contents and then flipping through the guide to obtain a quick overview. Topics of information are organized and presented in chapters, followed by workbook pages, which are differentiated from the other pages by the dark tabs in the right-hand corner.

The workbook pages are designed to be completed after reading the accompanying chapter. **In completing the activities on the workbook pages, parents have an opportunity to translate the theoretical material presented in the chapter into practical information about their own child.**

Also included are generous appendices, case studies, a list of additional resources, glossaries of terms and educational tests, and a list of references.

Parents who are new to the subject of learning disabilities may want to start with the first chapter and work through the book chapter by chapter. Experienced parents may instead want to skim chapters, reading in depth those of particular importance to them at this time. Completing the workbook pages throughout the book will provide an indication of how well one understands the information presented in the book—and one's own child's needs.

Using the Guide on an Ongoing Basis

The format of this book has been specifically designed to encourage parents to use the guide on an ongoing basis, instead of just reading it through once and putting it away on a bookshelf. The suggestions below will help to personalize the guide so that it does indeed become a working tool.

- After reading Chapter IV, "The LD Student at School" (in particular the section on keeping a file of your child's records, pp. 55–57), three-hole punch all of your child's evaluations, reports, etc., and file these in the oversize notebook. Follow the organizational tips described on p. 56 to set up this portion of the notebook.

  Use the tab dividers to reference your child's papers, e.g., "Test Reports," "IEPs," "Telephone Log," etc.

  Use the pocket folders to file irregularly-sized items such as report cards, teacher notes, etc. Label each pocket clearly.

- The workbook pages are perforated to provide for easy use. Remove workbook pages from the guide as you finish reading each chapter.

Prior to actually completing the workbook page, skim it briefly: it may be wise to photocopy some pages to provide additional blank forms for future use, while other pages may only be used one time.

- Complete each workbook page. This is your opportunity to apply your new knowledge and skills to *your* child (and that's why you're reading this book!).

- Once you have completed the various workbook pages, incorporate these pages (and any extra blank copies) into the appropriate section of your notebook file. For example, include your analysis of test reports (pp. 65–67) with your child's actual test reports; include the IEP checklists (pp. 69–78) with your child's IEP materials, and so on.

- Keep your notebook organized and up-to-date. Whenever you receive a new report, file it immediately. Don't succumb to the temptation to allow a stack of papers to accumulate, which you hope to file later.

- If your notebook has sufficient space, place your copy of *Understanding Learning Disabilities: A Parent Guide and Workbook* in the back, behind your youngster's reports, papers and your completed workbook pages. As you come across helpful written material about learning disabilities, perhaps from magazines, newspapers, parent groups, etc., make a copy of the material, three-hole punch it and file it in the back of your notebook with your guide. (As your child accumulates more reports and paperwork, you may need to have two notebooks: one for his paperwork and your completed workbook pages, and one for reference materials).

- Refer to your notebook often. Take it with you to all meetings with professionals about your child. You will have an immediate, personalized resource to which you can refer. Yes, it will take time and effort to organize it in the manner described. However, once you have set it up in this manner, it will prove to be an invaluable tool to you and your child—and, in the long run, it will save you much time and frustration.

- As you use the guide, you are encouraged to note additions and changes which you feel would make it more useful to parents. Your suggestions to the Council will be most welcome.

(If the above section, "Using the Guide on an Ongoing Basis," seems confusing or overwhelming now, don't worry! Read through the book and then re-read this section.)

Learning Disabilities Council
P.O. Box 8451
Richmond, Virginia 23226
(804) 748-5012

I. Learning Disabilities: The Hidden Handicap
A Basic Understanding

Who Can Have Specific Learning Disabilities

- Boys and girls
- All races
- All social and economic levels
- All ages

What Specific Learning Disabilities ARE

- Difficulties in acquiring, remembering, organizing, recalling, or expressing information
- Problems with reading, comprehension, writing, speaking, listening, and/or calculating. Rarely would a person show all the characteristics listed below; instead, there will be problems in one or more of the following areas:

    - *reading* – difficulty in remembering the printed word or symbol, figuring out words, reading with adequate speed, understanding what has been read

    - *writing* – poor penmanship, spelling, written composition

    - *speaking* – difficulty in making certain speech sounds, remembering names of things, organizing and sequencing ideas for verbal expression, speaking rhythmically

    - *listening* – difficulty remembering directions, understanding rapid speech, interpreting what is heard

    - *calculating* – problems remembering math facts such as multiplication tables, sequencing of steps, arithmetic processes, math signs (e.g., - + x < > ÷)

- A condition which may or may not be inherited; in some cases is acquired following neurological injury

- Good intelligence coupled with the inability to do some of the simplest tasks (e.g., tell right from left, recite the alphabet, memorize the multiplication tables). Historically, learning disabled individuals have been described as having "average or above intelligence." In recent years, however, there has been debate among professionals as to the inclusion of intelligence levels in a definition of learning disabilities.

What Specific Learning Disabilities Are NOT

- They are NOT primarily caused by any of the following:

    - visual, hearing, or motor handicaps (such as cerebral palsy)

    - mental retardation

    - emotional disturbance

    - environmental, cultural, or economic disadvantages

    - inappropriate instruction for that age and ability level

NOTE: Sometimes learning disabilities can coexist with other handicapping conditions. For example, while learning disabilities are not caused by emotional disturbance, a child may be both learning disabled **and** emotionally disturbed.

(*See* Appendix A for the federal and state definitions of Learning Disabilities. These are used by the public schools.)

What Learning Disabilities Are Like

Frustrating - Your child may look like everyone else but have difficulty doing what everyone else does.[1] This is why LD is often called the "Hidden Handicap."

Confusing - Your child may seem far ahead of others in some things but may be surprisingly inept in other skills. You may notice that your child does not seem to acquire or remember day-to-day bits of information which other children "naturally" seem to know.

Unique - Your child's combination and severity of problems may not be like those of anyone else you know.

How an LD Child is Often Described

● Lazy: "I know he could do better if he'd just work harder."

● Careless: "He can do it right; I know he can. He's so smart, but he just rushes through and makes careless mistakes."

● Doesn't try: "When he takes his time and really puts forth some effort, he can do the work. But most of the time, he just doesn't want to try hard enough."

● Unmotivated: "He couldn't care less about school. In fact, he isn't really interested in learning. He's just one of those unmotivated kids."

What Some of the Characteristics of LD Are

Everyone has his or her own learning strengths and weaknesses. As you read a list of learning disabilities characteristics, you may find a description or two that even sounds like something **you** do! To a certain extent, we all have **some** of the characteristics associated with those who are designated as "LD." The difference is in the number of characteristics that are demonstrated and the degree that they deviate from what is considered "normal." When the number and degree cause severe problems in the person's life (academically, vocationally, socially), that person may be considered learning disabled.

A list of characteristics usually found in such an individual is given in the chart which follows. It is important to remember that it would be unusual for an LD person to demonstrate all of these characteristics. It is far more likely that the person would have only a cluster of them—but to a degree that creates problems.

Examples of Learning Disability Characteristics [2,3]

NOTE: An individual need not demonstrate all of the following characteristics to be considered "LD." Rather, he will exhibit a cluster of difficulties to such a degree as to cause severe problems in daily living.

	Preschool	School Age	Adult
Sensory/Perceptual:	• may confuse words which sound the same: pin-pen, quiet-quite • may have trouble completing puzzles, seeing "fit" of pieces • may be unable to focus on what is being said by parent if radio or TV is audible in the background	• may make letter/number/word reversals (b-d, m-w, 6-9, was-saw) in reading and/or writing • may be confused by worksheets or pages crowded with print; may read "stilt" for "slit," "cover" for "clover," etc.; may lose place while reading • may be unable to focus on what teacher is saying if other students are talking in background, or an air conditioner or heater is making background noise	• may have trouble dialing phone numbers, reading addresses, route numbers; may reverse numbers in checkbook • may have difficulty reading the newspapers, following small print, columns, etc. • may have difficulty focusing on what employer is saying if office or factory machines are audible in background • may have trouble following a sewing pattern, construction diagram, etc.
Memory:	• seems to take a long time to learn information that others pick up quickly (names of colors, days of week, names of holidays, etc.) • may have difficulty providing information about self or family (age, birthday, number of brothers and sisters, etc.) • may lose train of thought; can't remember the topic of conversation if interrupted	• may forget books needed for homework, or forget to take completed homework to school • may have trouble following oral directions, particularly if several directions are given at one time • may have difficulty with rote memorization of spelling words, math facts, history dates, etc.	• may have difficulty learning new procedures and techniques at work if established routine is interrupted • may forget dates with friends or errands planned • may still lose train of thought; can't remember topic of conversation, if interrupted; may still have difficulty with multiplication tables, dates, etc.

	Preschool	School Age	Adult
Organization:	• bedroom may look like "disaster area" with belongings everywhere • may have difficulty perceiving patterns (e.g., trouble copying bead necklace, peg-board, or block patterns) • when given generalized instructions (e.g., "Get dressed"), may not know where or how to begin • may not understand the rules of games	• school desk and locker may be a "mess"—papers and books everywhere • even if reading is not a problem, may have difficulty with science and social studies due to problems with perceiving relationships among concepts and ideas • notebooks and notes may be incomplete, disjointed; doesn't know what's important to write down and what is not	• conversation may seem disjointed, with non sequiturs • may have difficulty telling or understanding jokes ("They just don't make sense.") • may constantly misplace belongings at work or home; seems bright, but like an "absent minded professor"
Spatial-Temporal Orientation:	• may have difficulty learning and understanding left-right, up-down, before-after, first-second, yesterday-tomorrow, etc. • may have difficulty gauging the edge of table in setting things down, causing frequent spills; bumps into objects when walking • may have difficulty telling a series of events in proper sequence, such as retelling a story or relating a TV show	• may work quickly, completing work in a rush but poorly; or may work slowly, with many incomplete assignments • may have difficulty in planning time in order to complete long-term assignments; may wait until last minute to study for tests • may have difficulty arranging work on paper—it may be cramped into small space or spread all over page • may have difficulty "lining up" numbers vertically, one under the other in math problems; may try to subtract the top number from bottom number, etc.	• may have difficulty following a schedule, planning time, being on time for appointments and deadlines; overestimates what can be accomplished in a given amount of time • may get lost easily, whether driving or trying to locate a room in a large building; may have difficulty reading maps • may have difficulty balancing a checkbook; doesn't "line up" numbers vertically, one under the other; may try to subtract the top number from the bottom number

	Preschool	School Age	Adult
Problem-solving:	• may have difficulty perceiving the relation-ship between actions and possible results or consequences (e.g., if you run with your cup of juice, it will spill on your shirt)	• may have difficulty learning the steps needed in more complicated math processes (multiplica-tion, division, algebraic equations) • after listening to part of a story, may have difficulty predicting what will happen next	• may have difficulty with brainstorming (i.e., thinking of different ways to do the same things); sees only one way to do something
Motor:	• may be clumsy, awkward, accident-prone • may have difficulty buttoning, tying , using scissors, catching or hitting a ball • may be much more active or much less active than other children	• may do poorly in sports requiring eye-hand coordination, such as baseball, tennis • may have difficulty learning to write; handwriting may be cramped or illegible • may be able to present information verbally, but cannot "get it down on paper," or takes an excessive amount of time to do so • may have difficulty copying from a book or the board, omitting letters or entire words	• may avoid hobbies like making models, woodworking, needle-point • may avoid writing whenever possible, preferring to dictate information for secre-tary or spouse to write
Language:	• may be slow in learning to talk • may confuse the order of sounds in words, saying "pasghetti" for "spaghetti," aminals" for "animals" • may forget the name for things; can describe the object, its use, etc., but cannot think of the name	• may have great diffi-culty learning to read, write, or spell • in reading, may have difficulty learning phonics; may read very slowly; may omit and substitute words while reading orally; may not understand what is read • may make spelling errors which are not even close to proper spelling; may include all the letters in a word, but in the wrong order; may spell the word correctly one time and then wrong several minutes later	• may still have difficulty saying longer words, confusing the order of sounds in words or phrases such as "episcopal," "statistics," "crisp biscuits" • may avoid reading, spelling, and writing whenever possible; may never read for pleasure • may have difficulty getting a job using capabilities because is unable to complete a job application correctly

	Preschool	School Age	Adult
Behavior/Social Skills:	• may exhibit sudden mood swings, such as bursts of rage when frustrated	• may have difficulty assessing own classroom performance; may think test grade will be high, but then is disappointed • teacher may say "appears immature"; may have difficulty making friends, or friends may be much younger	• may have difficulty interpreting body language, facial expressions, tone of voice, etc. leading to poor job performance and poor social relationships

General:	• may demonstrate uneven learning abilities, doing well in some things, but very poorly in others • may be able to learn information presented in one way, but not another; may learn what is seen but not what is heard; may remember what is practiced by writing, but not by reciting orally; may have difficulty with abstract ideas presented orally, if the concept they represent is not first presented 3-dimensionally • may have a short attention span, be impulsive, and/or easily distracted

Attention Deficit Disorders

Much has been written in recent years about ADD (Attention Deficit Disorders), which is also called ADHD (Attention Deficit Hyperactivity Disorders). It is a medical term applied to individuals who have significant difficulty in focusing and maintaining attention. While LD and ADD or ADHD are not the same, some LD people do suffer from both.

"ADHD is characterized by inattention, impulsivity and hyperactivity that is out of the normal range when compared with people of the same age. The behaviors include:

- often fidgets with hands and feet
- has difficulty remaining seated
- is easily distracted
- has difficulty awaiting turn
- often blurts out answer before the question has been completed
- has difficulty following instructions
- has difficulty sustaining attention
- often shifts from one uncompleted activity to another
- has difficulty playing quietly
- often talks excessively
- often interrupts
- often does not seem to listen
- often loses things
- often engages in dangerous activities without thinking of consequences"[4]

It is again important to point out that, at some time or other, nearly all children may exhibit one or two of the behaviors described above. The ADHD child, however, will exhibit many of these behaviors, day in and day out, over a long period of time.

If you think your child may be ADD or ADHD, you may wish to contact the organizations listed in Appendix B for more detailed information. Local mental health centers, as well as physicians and pediatric departments of area hospitals, may also be helpful in identifying parent support groups in your community.

[1]Virginia Association for Children & Adults with Learning Disabilities. *I'm not lazy...I want to; I'm not dumb...I try to; I'm not naughty...I need help; Maybe it's a learning disability.* Richmond, VA: Author.

[2]Nissenbaum, C. (1985). *The problem of learning disabilities – Dyslexia.* (2nd ed.) Chevy Chase, MD: Tri-Services, Inc. (Used with permission of the National Institute of Dyslexia.)

[3]Bright, G. and Trusdell, M. L. *Characteristics of learning disabilities.* Paper developed for the Learning Disabilities Council, Richmond, VA.

[4]American Psychiatric Association. (1987). *Diagnostic and statistical manual of mental disorders-Revised.* Washington, DC: Author.

Parent Observation

Instructions

To help prepare for school meetings and share your knowledge of your child, use the observation profile below to record the information. (Refer to the "Characteristics" chart on pages 3–6.)

Remember: Your observations are important in helping the school determine if learning problems do exist and what special services your child may need. Use this checklist to provide input for the initial referral, eligibility determination, and IEP development. (These steps in the special education process are described in detail in the Chapter "The LD Student at School.")

● Sensory/Perceptual

Does your child have trouble because of...

___making letter, number, word reversals?

___confusing similar letter sounds?

___other: _____

___other: _____

● Memory

Does your child have trouble...

___following a series of oral directions?

___retaining spelling words, math facts, history dates?

___other: _____

___other: _____

● Organization

Does your child have trouble...

___keeping school desk, notebook, and other belongings in order?

___understanding concepts in social studies and science?

___other: _____

___other: _____

● Spatial - Temporal Orientation

Does your child have trouble...

___arranging and spacing work on paper?

___learning left from right?

___other: _____

___other: _____

● Problem Solving

Does your child have trouble...

___predicting what will happen after hearing part of a story?

___figuring out different ways to accomplish a task?

___other: _____

___other: _____

● Motor

Does your child have trouble…

___in sports, seeming to be awkward?

___coloring, using scissors?

___other: _____

___other: _____

● Language

Reading

Does your child have trouble…

___sounding out words?

___remembering sight vocabulary (what, where, etc.)?

___recalling what has been read?

___other: _____

___other: _____

Writing

Does your child have trouble…

___copying?

___writing in manuscript or cursive?

___other: _____

___other: _____

Spelling

Does your child have trouble…

___memorizing spelling words?

___using these words later in sentences and paragraphs?

___other: _____

___other: _____

Listening

Does your child have trouble…

___following directions?

___interpreting what you say?

___other: _____

___other: _____

● Math

Does your child have trouble…

___remembering math facts?

___using math signs (+, -, <, >, etc.)?

___following a sequence of steps (as in long division)?

___other: _____

___other: _____

● Behavior/Social Skills

Does your child have trouble…

___focusing attention on one thing?

___interpreting body language, facial expressions?

___other: _____

___other: _____

II. Coping as a Parent

Parents' Feelings

"Exasperated ... Puzzled ... Uncertain ... Frantic ... Exhausted ... Helpless ... Sad ... Mad ... Hopeful. These are the feelings of the mother or father of a learning disabled child. He is bewildering. He drains parents and teachers. When they are with such a child, adults who are otherwise competent feel helpless and inadequate. Parents may feel very alone as they sense that friends and other family members do not understand what they are experiencing with the LD child.

"It's hard for any parents to accept the fact that they have a learning disabled child; for some it becomes an almost overwhelming tragedy.

"There are stages that parents go through with their perfectly normal looking, intelligent child, who doesn't learn or behave as other children his age do. A whole gamut of emotions must be faced before parents can grapple effectively with the stark truth of a child having learning disabilities. There is no set order to these feelings. Usually they start with denial and, most often, end with acceptance and hope."[1]

DENIAL...FLIGHT...ISOLATION...GUILT...ANGER...BLAME...

FEAR...ENVY...BARGAINING...DEPRESSION...MOURNING...

ACCEPTANCE...HOPE

"OK. So he's got learning disabilities.

What can I do to help?

How can I make him feel better about himself?

What are his strengths?

What are his interests?

We'll make it! It will just take time and some cooperative efforts."[2]

Feelings of Guilt

Try to overcome any guilt feelings you may have. It is useless to take or place blame. Evidence is building to suggest that learning disabilities may be inherent in a child's biological make-up. You, no doubt, have always done your best with the information you have had at the time. Dwelling on the past will not help. Use your past experiences to guide present and future decisions.

Importance of Having a Confidant

Having a confidant may help. Being able to talk with someone—one's spouse, a family member, or a close friend—who is a good listener and has an interest in your child may provide support and comfort. If this is unsatisfactory to you, it might be wise to seek the professional help of a licensed professional counselor, a school psychologist or licensed clinical psychologist, or a licensed clinical social worker. (See the glossary for definitions of these professionals.)

Parent Support Groups

Parent support groups and meetings of the local chapters of organizations such as the Learning Disabilities Association of America (LDAA) are another source of comfort and of practical advice; contact the national office for information on the chapter in your area. (See Appendix B for more information).

In many localities, parent training and information centers, where parents of handicapped children assist and provide information to other parents, have been established. (See Appendix C for state-by-state listings).

You may discover other resources in your area by contacting: teachers of the learning disabled in local public and private schools, the special education department for teacher training in any nearby colleges or universities, mental health centers, the pediatrics department of area hospitals and United Way Information and Referral Services.

Learning About LD

Reading about learning disabled individuals provides hope as well as worthwhile information (see Case Studies and Additional Reading). Indeed, it is important to learn all that you can about learning disabilities and about your own child's pattern of strengths and weaknesses. One expert has suggested that "lack of information leads to anxiety and guilt in the family and to low self-esteem" in the child. He says that knowledge changes family attitudes and leads to greater sympathy and understanding of the LD individual.[3]

Being an Advocate for Your Child

The LD child needs an advocate. **You know your child better than anyone else**. Learn as much as you can about your youngster's strengths and weaknesses, unique learning style, and special needs. If, in spite of your love, interest and knowledge, you feel inadequate for the task of advocacy, find someone who will champion your child for you, possibly a teacher, a coach, a counselor, an educational consultant, a psychologist (again, refer to the glossary), or one of the groups listed in Appendix B.

If you do decide to undertake the role of advocate for your child, it should be with the realization that this is not a skill you will learn and then use for a year or two. Parents of LD children need to acknowledge that they will be the person (usually the only person) who has the overall picture of their child's disability, not only at a single point in time but throughout the years. You will find yourself playing the role of facilitator, coordinator, and overseer—no matter how good your child's school program and no matter how competent the professionals working with your child.

It's much better to undertake the job realizing that it's a long-term commitment that will demand the best of your skills and energy than to approach the situation with the idea that your responsibility will be to find the right school and the right teacher, and, that done, you will be able to relax while others take over.

The "light at the end of the tunnel" will approach as you gradually teach your youngster to be his or her own advocate. Some of the greatest gifts parents can give their LD teenager as they move through the upper grades are the confidence and skills to speak up in order to secure the accommodations needed: more time to complete a test, shorter assignments, help in taking lecture notes, etc.

It's a fine line the parent must learn to walk between providing enough support so the LD teenager doesn't flounder and teaching the student "learned helplessness," a situation certainly to be avoided.

Being an Advocate for Learning Disabled Individuals

At some point, you may recognize that the difficulties which you have faced or are facing with your LD child are similar to those faced by other parents of LD children. Perhaps problems exist within the system—possibly a school or a school system or legislation, etc.—which impact upon many learning disabled individuals, but are beyond the grasp of one parent to change.

You may wish to join other parents and professionals to advocate for specific policy changes in a given system. For example, you may feel there is a need for regular classroom teachers to receive additional training and support to enable them to integrate children with varying needs, including learning disabilities, into the regular classroom. This type of system-wide change is not something that one parent can hope to accomplish alone. However, by joining groups such as your school system's Special Education Advisory Committee or the local affiliates of the Learning Disabilities Association of America (*see* Appendix B), you can begin to advocate for systematic policy changes affecting all learning disabled individuals.

Some parents may find this type of advocacy overwhelming while their own child seems to require so much of their attention. Other parents find it stimulating and rejuvenating.

Structure

Maintaining structure in the home makes things smoother and easier for all members of the family. Life runs more smoothly, too, if both parents can agree on strategies for handling discipline.

Communication

When you feel bad about an unfortunate incident, your child probably feels worse and needs love and acceptance. Make a conscious effort to keep the lines of communication open. Listen carefully to what your youngster says and be aware of the signals given through body language and actions. Let your child know what makes you feel happy. Try to prepare him or her for the consequences of impulsive and inappropriate actions.

Importance of a Sense of Humor

Try to maintain a sense of humor. It can be a great release when tensions build. It can enable you to help your child examine the hurts and reduce the pain. Humor is a great therapist!

Live one day at a time and focus on the positive aspects of your life and on each small success of your child.

A note to the primary caretaker, mother or father:

Find time to be alone. You need time to relax and to think. If possible, make time for your favorite relaxation technique, whether it's with a good book, a hot tub, or quiet music. Set aside a time to engage in your favorite hobby without interruption. In addition, make an effort to get away with your spouse for an occasional weekend together. If it's inconvenient or too costly to get a baby-sitter for that time, try to get another parent with whom you can reciprocate to keep your child or children for the weekend.

Perhaps this "Bill of Rights for Parents of Handicapped Children" says it best:

Bill of Rights for Parents of Handicapped Children[4]

Freedom To ...

Feel that you have done the best you can.

Enjoy life as intensely as possible, even though you have a handicapped child.

Let your handicapped child have his or her own privacy.

Have hostile thoughts once in a while without feeling guilty.

Enjoy being alone at times.

Have a two-week vacation yearly without the children; have dates, celebrations, weekends away, time together to enhance your marriage.

Say at times you don't want to talk about your problems. Say, "I'm tired of talking about my handicapped child."

Lie once in a while. Say everything is fine.

Don't feel compelled to tell the truth to everyone who asks.

Tell your child you don't like certain things he does, even though you've been told to offer much praise.

Devote as much time as you want to the handicapped cause; get away for a while and return if you want.

Tell teachers and professionals what you really feel about the job they are doing; demand they respect your opinions.

Tell people about your child's progress and achievements with a real sense of pride.

Have your own hobbies and interests.

Spend a little extra money on yourself, even though you feel you can't afford it.

Warning: Parents who do not enjoy almost all of these freedoms are in trouble. Martyrs are seldom appreciated by anybody.

[1]Fried, H. (1979). *Plain talk about children with learning disabilities.* Washington, DC: U.S. Department of Health, Education and Welfare, p. 3.

[2]*Ibid.*, p. 4.

[3]Rosenthal, J. H. (1973). *Hazy? Crazy? and/or Lazy?* San Rafael, CA: Academic Therapy Publications.

[4]Gordon, S. *A survival guide for people who have handicaps.* Syracuse, NY: Institute for Family Research and Education.

III. Helping Your Child At Home

If your child is learning disabled or if, after you've read the first chapter, you suspect that your child may be learning disabled, you are no doubt wondering what you can do to make life better for the youngster. While your child does indeed spend a large percentage of time each day in school, it is important to recognize the significance of those activities which occur out of the school environment. Furthermore, it is in this area, i.e., the home and family, that you as a parent can have a direct, immediate influence. This chapter will be devoted to helping you help your child at home while the following chapter will focus on the school environment.

Self Esteem

Signs of Weak Self-Esteem

Does your youngster show several of the following traits?

- Difficulty in accepting being wrong; it is always someone else's fault

- Excessive blaming of self for inadequacies, "I knew I wouldn't do it right" or, at the opposite extreme, satisfaction with inadequate performance

- Difficulty in making decisions and insecurity about own ideas

- Excessive need for acceptance, with a great desire to please those in authority

- Self-consciousness, with a minimizing of accomplishments

- Difficulty in accepting responsibility or over-acceptance of responsibility (trying to continually prove self)

- Overly dependent

If so, your child may be having difficulty with self-esteem—with feeling worthy.

A feeling of self-worth affects our thinking processes, our emotions, desires, values, and goals; therefore, it underlies our every behavior. Children with low self-esteem often suffer from feelings of frustration and helplessness. They may feel angry and depressed. Children with high self-esteem feel confident and effective. They can interact assertively with their own environment and feel self-assured about making decisions.[1]

Suggestions for Improving Self-Esteem

Self-esteem begins to develop early, so it is important for parents and other family members to provide experiences and promote attitudes that build a child's feeling of being a worthy person, long before the child starts school.

How do we accomplish this? How do we let our LD children know that we accept them as they are and promote their feelings of self-esteem? Some suggestions follow:

- Speak openly and honestly with your child. Acknowledge that there are problems but accentuate the positives. Let your child know that having trouble in school does not mean failure in life.

- Listen to your child. Communication is a two-way process. Don't feel as if you need to come up with the answer or know what is best. Often our children just want to know we understand them.

- Communicate your love without words, too. Touch is a real human need.

- Maintain a sense of humor. Catastrophes of today are often what wonderful stories are made of in the years to come.

- Allow autonomy, independence, and self-reliance to grow. Give your child time to be alone, and to take as much responsibility for self-care and self-satisfaction as possible. Don't step in when you aren't needed. This establishes the connection between one's own actions and one's own comfort or happiness.

- Help your child to experience success. Sometimes a youngster will need guidance in learning a task or skill. In providing the guidance, build on your child's strengths and competencies so success will follow. Break tasks down into small steps. It is important that excessive frustration and failure be avoided. Acknowledge your child's **efforts** towards a goal, not just the **achievement** of a goal.

- Do allow your child to experience **some** frustration. Frustration tolerance is important in meeting the challenges to be encountered in life. If you protect children too much from failure or frustration, then they will fail to learn proper coping strategies. A child needs to develop the concept of himself as a person who can fail without losing self-confidence and self-respect.

- Help your child to set realistic goals. Often those with negative, low self-concepts set their goals either unrealistically high or unrealistically low. Unfortunately, this is self-reinforcing and they continue to act consistently with their self-concept.

- Help your child to label feelings and describe experiences. This promotes self-awareness and self-control because understanding which feeling is being experienced is the first step towards dealing with it.

Home as a Haven

In leading an LD child to an honest acceptance and understanding of his or her own disability, parents must be sure that they and any other family members do not get in the habit of making comments which would encourage a feeling of guilt or shame for something for which the LD youngster is not to blame. **The youngster's home should be the one place in the world where understanding and encouragement can be found.** Unless all members of the family work toward this goal, the child may develop strong feelings of guilt and worthlessness.

Convincing an LD child that he or she is not stupid is always a long process. It cannot be accomplished by a speech that is made only once. Day by day things happen that make LD youngsters feel dumb, such as forgetting to finish chores assigned at home; or always being the last one chosen for a team in the neighborhood ball game because of clumsiness in catching and hitting the ball; or spending three hours studying for a test, then flunking it flat; or misreading "ask" as "ass" right in front of the whole class; or being suspended from high school because the youngster ripped up the Shakespeare textbook and threw it at the English teacher's feet. As such situations arise, the child will need help getting over the hurt feelings, anger, and embarrassment. There will be a need to have someone calmly help the youngster figure out which LD symptoms caused the problem, how that particular problem is different from really being generally "dense," and how to avoid letting the problem lead to another bad situation in the future.[2]

The importance of self-esteem in a child's life can hardly be overemphasized. It is the mainspring that launches every child toward success or failure as a human being. Because children begin to generate their own ideas of their self-worth during the early years, it is important that we know how to nurture and support this process.[3]

[1]Frank, R. (1985). Self-esteem building. *Interact*, April, 1985, pp. 4–5.

[2]Stevens, S. (1980). *The learning disabled child: Ways that parents can help.* Winston-Salem, NC: John F. Blair Publishers, pp. 84—85.

[3]Frank, R. (1985). *op. cit.*

Extracurricular Activities

Suggested Activities

Finding an area of competence outside academic subjects provides an ego boost for a child who does not feel good about the way things are going in the classroom. The youngster may gain status among peers through collecting rocks or becoming the neighborhood ornithologist or becoming a karate expert or excelling in art or music. Such activities should be encouraged, even if it means somewhat less time for studying.[1]

As a parent, you know your child best. Let your youngster's interests guide you in helping to find activities in which he or she can succeed. If your child is physically strong and well coordinated, team sports such as football and basketball can be great. But not all LD children have the eye-hand coordination needed to handle a ball and keep up with their peers in competitive team sports. In that case, they need opportunities to try such things as swimming, gymnastics, bowling, boating, climbing, hiking, karate, horseback riding, skiing, archery, or fencing. Swimming especially may be a sport at which learning disabled youngsters may excel as no eye–hand coordination is required. In tennis and golf it is usually possible to find other individuals at one's own level of skill with whom to play; however, the difficulty with hand-eye coordination may make tennis a poor choice. LD youngsters who have the opportunity to ride horses and to sail often find these especially appealing.

Some LD children become adept at games of strategy, such as chess, backgammon, bridge, or pinochle. Playing these well can be ego-strengthening and a source of lifetime pleasure.

Give your child opportunities to explore—to find those activities at which he or she can be successful. Don't become upset if your youngster tries one kind of extracurricular activity and then drops it and moves on to another. What **is** important is for each child to find that which brings the most satisfaction. As with all youngsters, LD young people like to do those things at which they can succeed, and they will want to continue

to be involved in the activities which make them feel good about themselves.

Resources

Private or group instruction in voice, piano, band instruments, and all facets of dance is generally available in most communities, with categorical listings in the "yellow pages" of the local phone directory. Additional opportunities in these areas, as well as in art and drama, may be available through the fine arts and performing arts departments of nearby colleges and universities. Likewise, museums often offer special workshops on topics of particular interest to children. In addition, a national program, Very Special Arts, promotes participation in all the arts by children with special needs. (Write to Very Special Arts, The John F. Kennedy Center for the Performing Arts, Washington, DC 20566 for information in your area.)

For students with an interest in the outdoors, activities may be available though 4-H clubs, local garden clubs, area parks or botanical gardens.

If your youngster has an interest in a special craft, photography, or even computers, the adult education department of your local schools may be helpful in identifying individuals who may be able to work with your child. Perhaps a friend or acquaintance would be willing to share a special hobby.

Boy Scouts and Girl Scouts offer an excellent outlet for the tremendous energy that many LD children have. It structures their time and teaches them useful skills in

[1]Osman, B. (1984). Spotting problems and setting a course. *New York Times Fall Survey,* November 11, 1984, Section 12, p. 46.

an atmosphere that can be non-threatening. Look in the "white pages" of your phone book or check with area schools or churches to locate a group near you.

Opportunities to participate in organized sports activities generally abound. Check with your community recreation department, schools, and YMCA.

Summer camping may be another option to consider. You may wish to consult the directory of camps published by the American Camping Association (1-800-428-CAMP).

Explaining LD

Do remember to alert those who will work with your child that some special care may need to be taken, such as giving oral instructions slowly and clearly, giving extra help when referring to right or left, providing ample encouragement at every step in the learning process, and not asking your youngster to read orally. Or you may have a different set of suggestions that apply to your son or daughter. This may be the first time that this Sunday School teacher or Scout leader has had anyone explain the special needs of an LD individual.

Family Involvement

Helping the Whole Family

There are both practical and emotional issues with which a family must cope when a child has a learning disability. The educational decisions and special arrangements, the financial strain, the disappointments and frustrations all create pressures on the entire family.[1]

Even so, it is vital that the family find ways of demonstrating its acceptance of its LD child and of working together. Not only does the youngster need help—the whole family needs help.

Many of the suggestions for helping an LD child will also help the other children in the home, thereby also helping the parents. So, it is not a question of treating your LD child one way while you have entirely different expectations for the other children. The following suggestions can apply to most children, depending upon their ages.

● Be firm, consistent, and explicit.

Clear, concise, consistent expectations prevent confusion, insecurity, and misunderstanding. For example, "There are to be no other people in this house unless I am home" is clearer and more concise than "I would prefer that you not have other people in the house unless I'm home." The consistency will come when you repeat the instructions each time you leave home, and make no exceptions.[2]

● Give your child a voice in major decision-making processes.

If a very important decision must be made, listen to your child's opinions and the reasons for them. It's not that the final decision rests with the youngster, but that you are showing respect by listening to those opinions. It also encourages the child to think logically and then to articulate those thoughts aloud.[3]

● Assign chores around the house.

This helps the child to feel a part of the family; it also teaches responsibility and specific skills often particularly needed by LD youngsters: fine and gross motor control, sequencing, and memory.

There are some points to remember when assigning chores, the first being that chores are easy to forget, so reminders are helpful. For youngsters who can read adequately, lists can be taped to the refrigerator door or bulletin board. Pictures or simple line-drawings can be used for youngsters with inadequate reading skills. Charts are also useful. A pencil attached with a string enables the youngster to check off the chores as they are completed.

If chores aren't done even after many reminders, privileges may have to be withheld. But make it clear ahead of time that if a chore goes undone, a privilege will be withheld.

Check on the completed chore. If it's been done incorrectly, praise whatever portion was done properly and correct gently.[4] There is a caution about evaluating the chores completed by the LD youngster: applying the same criteria of neatness or responsibility as are applied to a brother or sister may not be realistic or fair. The LD youngster should be evaluated as an individual, not necessarily with expectations identical to those for the siblings.[5]

● Establish a regular routine at home.

Clearly established routines reduce confusion and anxiety—for all in the family. We all feel more secure when we know what to expect.

Not this!

With the child's input, you may want to write the daily schedule on a chart. An example follows:

6:30	Get up Dress Make bed
7:00	Breakfast Brush teeth
7:30	Leave for school
3:30	Return from school; snack Free time
5:15	Chores
5:45	Homework
6:30	Dinner
7:15	Complete homework
8:30	Bedtime [6]

The last three suggestions, which follow below, apply particularly to the LD youngster.

● Be direct, brief, and supportive.

Say what you expect in simple, easy terms, with a pleasant and encouraging tone of voice. Be as concrete as possible when you ask the youngster to do something.

For many who have trouble following directions, it is helpful to remind, "Look at my face while I speak." If you are not sure the child understands, ask him or her—gently—to repeat what you said. But if you are still not sure you've gotten through to your child, suggest a demonstration of what you asked for. Remember, be positive; support and direct, rather than criticize.[7]

● Simplify; reduce stimulation.

Simplify family routine. If mealtime is particularly stimulating in your home, your LD child may react by becoming irritable. If this happens, the youngster may need an "escape route," perhaps being allowed to leave the table—not ordered to. Or to eat earlier than the rest of the family.

Your LD child's room should be a retreat, a place for relaxation. If a separate room is not possible, consider screening off a part of a room with a folding screen or tall piece of furniture.

To reduce clutter, keep as many possessions as possible on closet shelves or in drawers. For younger LD children, you may have to store some toys for a few weeks, then exchange them for the toys that have been out a while.[8]

● Provide as few alternatives as possible in decision-making situations.

Numerous choices can be confusing and overwhelming to an LD youngster. Fewer alternatives presented usually bring about quicker and easier decisions.[9]

Helping the LD Youngster Learn

● Non-Academic Skills

"Parents can make mealtime, bedtime, a drive in the car, a trip to the supermarket and ordinary household activities into meaningful teaching situations. . . . Involvement in the life of the household gives a feeling of competence that can help to counteract the sense of failure instilled by low marks," writes Margaret Golick in *A Parent's Guide to Learning Problems.* Many parents of LD youngsters have become skilled at using day-to-day experiences in teaching their children order, logic, arithmetic, and improved language skills.[10] For example, cutting an orange into halves, the halves into quarters (or "fourths") and the quarters into eighths can be a hands-on, enlightening lesson in fractions. For younger children, playing "store" with items from the pantry, using play money, can teach not only money value but also counting by fives and tens.

● Academic Skills

Tutoring of an LD child by Mother or Dad is usually the beginning of misery for both parent and child. It is indeed a rare parent—even one who is a good teacher of academic subjects for other children—who can be an effective tutor for his or her own child. The problem is that when the mother-child or father-child relationship is converted to a teacher-child relationship, both the parent and the child are too emotionally involved to remain objective and "neutral."[11] Then anger flares; guilt and fear follow. Instead of one suffering LD child, we now have a miserable family.[12] There is a better way.

Some suggestions follow:

(1) As much as possible, avoid sitting down to work **with** your LD child.

Set up a study place in his or her room or some other quiet part of the house where there is the least likelihood of being disturbed. Then when help is needed, if possible have the youngster come to someone for assistance, then return to the study area to work alone. If the learning disability is severe enough that this would not be practical, set up a study place near enough to the person helping so the youngster won't have to leave the desk or make someone come to it.

If you find you **do** have to sit down with your child, set limits before you start, based on your review of the work that must be completed that evening.[13] You might say, "You have ten social studies questions to answer? OK, I'll read the questions to you, then you answer as many as you can on the tape recorder, by yourself, while I'm fixing dinner. After dinner you can write them down; then I'll go over what you've written. After that you can make any changes that are needed, by yourself."

(2) Set time limits on homework.

Consult with your youngster's teacher or teachers concerning the amount of time that should be needed to complete the assigned homework. It could very well be that the amount of time suggested by the teacher won't be adequate for **your** LD youngster, depending upon the severity of the learning disability, the speed with which the child normally works, the amount of "drive" in the personality, and other factors. If so, you can help the youngster understand that reality says that he or she is going to have to spend more time on homework than some of the others in the class.

However, if you find that your youngster is spending so much time on homework that there isn't an adequate amount of time for recreation and socializing, this

should be discussed with the teacher. Perhaps some adjustment can be made in the **number** of problems assigned, or the **length** of the essay to be written. There's no reason that every child in the class should have an identical assignment, **as long as the appropriate learning of the concept or principle takes place**. Even so, you'll find that this is a difficult concept for some teachers to accept. Before approaching the teacher with this idea, you should have had sufficient conversations with the teacher that he or she understands how your child functions academically.

(3) Be aware that you may need to change the extent of help given.

Sometimes, because of habit, parents will continue to provide direct assistance to a child with a subject that is difficult even though the youngster has reached the point where it could be done alone. Perhaps only a quick check by the parent **after** the work is completed will suffice.[14]

(4) The person who provides help does not have to be one of the child's parents. However, in choosing the best possible person, three qualifications must be considered:

– Most important, the helper must be able to work peacefully with the child. Sarcasm, harsh criticism, arguing, sulking, tears, or shouting mean that the wrong person has been chosen.

– College degrees or high school diplomas are not as important as empathy, ability to clarify confusing points, and intelligence.

– Anyone forced into the job is likely to have the wrong attitude. Older siblings are often the worst possible choices.[15]

Do remember that although it is not advisable for parents to tutor their child directly, it is important that they remain informed about the child's classroom performance and progress—or lack of it.

To summarize, the family should support, encourage, and appreciate each other. Your LD child will then be able to reflect this strengthening kind of love. The greatest gift parents can give their children is a home life that teaches them they are valued and are contributing members of the family. These are more important lessons to be learned than spelling, multiplication tables, and how to write neatly.[16]

[1] Osman, B. (1987). Learning disabilities: A family affair. *Their World*. New York: Foundation for Children with Learning Disabilities.

[2] Rozantes, P. (1981). Hints for a happier home. *The Observer,* February 1981, p. 7.

[3] *Ibid.*

[4] *Ibid.*

[5] Osman, B. (1987). *op. cit*, p. 11.

[6] Rozantes, P. (February 1981). *op. cit.*

[7] Brutten M., Richardson, S. O., and Mangel, C. (1973). *Something's wrong with my child*. New York: Harcourt Brace Jovanovich, p. 136.

[8] Brutten et al. (1973). *op. cit.*, pp. 137–138.

[9] Rozantes, P. (February 1981). *op. cit.*

[10] Brutten et. al. (1973). *op. cit.*, pp. 126–127.

[11] Brutten et al. (1973). *op. cit.*, p. 127.

[12] Stevens, S. H. (1980). *The learning disabled child: Ways that parents can help*. Winston-Salem, North Carolina: John F. Blair Publishers, pp. 84–85.

[13] Stevens, S. H. (1980). *op. cit.*, p. 96.

[14] Stevens, S. H. (1980). *op. cit.*, p. 98.

[15] Stevens, S. H. (1980). *op. cit.*, pp. 99–100.

[16] Brutten et al. (1973). *op. cit.*, pp. 141–142.

Discipline

Parent's Response to The Child

In some families, an interaction cycle has developed between parent and LD child that is almost invariably negative: the child's behavior elicits a negative response from the parent, and in turn the parent's negative feedback elicits further negative behavior from the youngster.

A new attitude on the part of the parent is needed to break this cycle.

The first step may be for the parent to realize that the LD child's behavior is not always under the youngster's control. It is not purposefully designed to "get" you. As a part of the disability, the LD child may lack the inner controls needed to modify impulsive and "driven" behavior.[1]

Child's Response

The second step is to help the youngster accept responsibility for the problem, understand what made it happen, and work toward a solution. This will not happen if the first step has not taken place—if the child feels blamed or perceives your anger, which just generates more negative behavior, thus restarting the cycle. It also delays the child's acceptance of responsibility for the problem; this would be too painful for the youngster if the atmosphere is full of blame and punishment.

An example would be spilled milk. Despite numerous warnings about pouring milk too fast, impulsive kids will often forget and spill. A parent's earlier anger will not prevent this from happening once again. Instead, you might observe, "You forgot the rule about pouring too fast. What do you need to do to fix the problem?"

Together, parents and child can then generate solutions which may include an apology, some sponging-up by the youngster, and a contribution from the allowance toward replenishing the wasted milk. Remember to attack the situation—not the child.

This procedure helps the child to feel responsible but not blamed and to feel he or she is making a contribution to restitution which tends to relieve guilt. At the same time the parent has an alternative to placing blame and generating anger.[2]

Another example is leaving a textbook or school papers at home. After many reminders, your teenager continues to leave at home a textbook needed in class. Instead of ineffective nagging, establish a routine by which the student forms the habit of placing all school books and supplies (and lunch!) in front of the door used when leaving for school the next morning.

Handling Anger

Many adults will say to the LD youngster, "You shouldn't feel so angry." But the child has a right to feel angry. How would you respond if you had a problem that made you look stupid and kept you from doing many of the things you wanted to do? Of course you'd get angry—just as your child does.

Admittedly it's not just the anger itself that parents respond to. It's what the youngster does with the anger that can cause trouble. So someone is needed to help the child figure out what to do with the anger in order to get rid of it. And the way to get rid of it is to express it—in some way that does not harm. This is something that LD youngsters often must be taught.

When a youngster's anger gets out of control, many parents use Time Out, a method of removing the child from the situation and allowing time to cool off or calm down in the privacy of the child's own room or other isolated area. This isolation, however, should not be viewed by either the child or the parent as punishment. If the order, "Go to your room!" is accompanied by the parent's anger, this may be interpreted by the child as rejection and punishment. Instead, instruct your child in a manner that communicates that this is the best place to be at this moment to relax and reflect on how to handle similar situations in the future.

If your child fights a lot:

– If you are angry, express how you feel about your child's behavior but state that your love hasn't changed.

– Listen to your child's side of the story, but also have him or her play the other role to feel the other person's feelings.

– Explore alternatives to aggressive behavior and role play them.

– Establish a reward system, e.g., the child will earn a reward for a day without fighting.

Consistency

Most children—learning disabled or not—become more manageable when their parents are consistent with discipline. But it is admittedly hard to be consistent, and almost impossible to be so all the time. The trick is to be as consistent as possible.

Learning disabled youngsters are often uncertain how to behave; therefore, they use the models around them for their own behavior. If you value a certain kind of behavior, don't just advocate it; use it **yourself**. That's what your LD youngster will learn. If you behave consistently, your child is more apt to behave consistently.[3]

Punishment

When you punish, try to be fair, calm, and prompt. Pediatrician George W. Brown, in an article in the *Journal of Learning Disabilities*, says, "Delay causes the child to be confused about what he did wrong [and] gives the child a long period of worry and resentment."[4] He adds other suggestions:

● Let the punishment fit the crime. Don't impose a major punishment for a minor infraction.

● Don't punish the same behavior with widely different penalties at different times.

● Avoid long sermons, talk, logical reasoning. Make the handling of the problem direct and simple.

● Don't demand verbal assurances from the youngster that such a thing will never happen again.

● Try to avoid punishments that are violent or lead to great excitement. Don't let your own feelings of anger and frustration distort the situation.

● Make clear to the child that you dislike his action, not him. The youngster needs an improved self-image, not degradation.

● Avoid threats, bribes, or promises. Harsh criticism is sometimes more inflammatory than instructive.

● Avoid being too strict and then too forgiving—cold anger at one time and then loving embraces soon after.

● Hold you temper if you want your LD child to learn that temper can be held.[5]

[1]Pastor, D. (1986). Self-control therapy with learning disabled children. *ACLD Newsbriefs*. January/February 1986. Pittsburgh, PA: Association for Children and Adults with Learning Disabilities.

[2]Ibid.

[3]Brutten, M., Richardson, S.O., and Mangel, C. (1973). *Something's wrong with my child.* New York: Harcourt Brace Jovanovich, p. 134.

[4]Ibid. p. 131.

[5]Ibid. p. 132.

Interpersonal Relationships

The Family

Problems arise in all families, but with LD children the problems may be more intense. The youngster may feel hated by siblings, and the brothers and sisters may feel that their parents favor the LD child because of the extra time and attention required for the problems that arise from the disability.[1]

Brothers and sisters are going to disagree and fight. Parents, however, must see to it that the LD child's disability is not allowed to become a special target for insults.[2] They can assert, "No one in this family is dumb or stupid!"

It is up to the parents to help all family members—not only siblings, but also aunts and uncles, cousins, and grandparents—to understand the nature of learning disabilities and that the LD youngster is not being deliberately difficult.

Other Children

There are several things that parents can do to improve the way their LD child interacts with others:

● Observe your child.

Try to figure out what your child does that is different from the children who have successful interpersonal relationships. As you observe, state to yourself what the specific behavior is.[3] For example, say "Billy got mad, grabbed his football and walked off when his side began to fall behind in a touch-football game," rather than "Billy won't share his belongings."

You might find it worthwhile to keep a written record of your observations—not to confront Billy with, but to help you understand how Billy behaves differently, in general. Ask yourself, "What does my child do or not do that causes problems? When does this happen? Why? What are possible motives?"[4]

● Structure the environment for success.

Failures in peer relationships can frequently be avoided through careful planning. For example, when your youngster's friends have been invited over, have the snack ready (your child can help

with this), and discuss ahead of time what game will be played or what activity would be most enjoyed. Also plan with your child the length of the visit, so the friends can leave before there is time for failures. Rehearse the *dos* and *don'ts* of being a good friend. If your child is going to have a party, encourage the child to help with the planning. Consider serving refreshments—either at your home or at a snack shop—and then taking the group to the movies or a special entertainment (e.g., an ice-skating show, or a basketball game). Rehearse the entire schedule beforehand so your child knows what to expect.

Some LD children "roll with the punches" better than others. Some need prior preparation for an upcoming event. Change in schedule or environment is not easy for many LD children. Even such family events as dinner parties, vacations, and weekend visits by relatives or friends are handled better by the LD child if the youngster is prepared in advance and is told what to expect. Role-playing situations and making suggestions as to how to act or what to say might give the LD child greater confidence when facing a new situation or change in his routine.

● Work out a signal system.

Many youngsters respond well to having a "secret" signal system or code word to help remind the child that he needs to stop, breathe, and relax for a moment—that the situation is beginning to get out of hand. The signal might be a wink, a finger on the nose, etc.

● Replay the "moment."

After an unpleasant experience, it is worthwhile to work on the problem. However, do not try to do this while your youngster is still upset.

Rather than setting out the problem as you see it, or accusing, let your child problem-solve and role-play in order to arrive at some alternative ways for handling such a problem in the future. Be sure that your child plays the other person's role in order to feel how the other person felt.

● If your child isolates himself or herself:

– Enroll the child in structured activities that the child is comfortable with (e.g., art lessons, Scouting, etc.).

– Help with peer contact by suggesting activities: going skating, baking at home with a friend, having a small party.

– Do not push your child too quickly. It is necessary to build confidence first. Success builds more success.

– Suggest that your child practice ways of meeting new friends: Walk up to the person standing alone. Let the other person talk about himself or herself. Look the person in the eye and listen well. Rehearse conversation starters. Use open-ended questions, e.g., "Tell me more!"

● Praise efforts.

Be sure to give your child positive feedback when you notice that he or she is trying to make positive changes.[5]

[1] Sternberg, W. Self-esteem and your learning disabled child. *HELP*. Arkansas ACLD Newsletter.

[2] Stevens, S. H. (1980). *The learning disabled child: Ways that parents can help*. Winston-Salem, North Carolina: John F. Blair Publishers.

[3] White, S. Building social skills and self-esteem; How parents can help. Minnesota ACLD Newsletter.

[4] Ibid.

[5] Ibid.

Self Esteem

Everyone Needs
Support and Encouragement

Instructions

At the end of the day, sit down by yourself to think about your interactions with your child on this particular day. Using the checklist which follows, check off those descriptions which best describe your behaviors.

Review the checklist. Overall, did you interact in such a way as to build your child's self-esteem? Choose one or two items and make a conscious effort during the next day (or week) to act in such a way as to enhance your child's confidence. If necessary, jot yourself reminders on "post-it" sticky notes and place them in visible places to help you remember. At the end of this time period, use the checklist and a different color pen to reassess your interaction. Then set new goals; select new items to emphasize, and repeat the process.

Use the checklist from time to time to check on how you're doing.

How Am I Doing?

	Yes, I did it	No, I forgot	Sometimes I thought about it	I need to work on it
Today, I have …				
• told him that I love him				
• hugged him				
• praised him (there are lots of ways to say "good". I said _____)				
• laughed **with** him, not **at** him				
• asked him to tell me one good thing that happened today				
• given him special jobs to do (and praised him for completing them)				
• spent time alone with him				
• allowed him to do what he could do for himself (zipped zippers, gathered school materials, _____)				
• really listened to what he said				
• **helped** him solve a problem rather than **telling** what is best to do				
• made sure that he has been successful at something (since school is not always great)				
• told someone else something positive about him and made sure that he heard me				
• encouraged **him** to tell the teacher when he is having trouble (to always intervene tells him that he is inadequate)				
• encouraged extracurricular activities in which he can succeed				

Special Assignment For Homework Success

Instructions: Before reading the next several pages, jot down problems or concerns you have noted with regard to your child's homework and schoolwork.

_____

_____

_____

_____

_____

_____

_____

_____

_____

_____

_____

_____

_____

_____

_____

_____

_____

Now refer to the suggestions which follow to help make the homework experience less painful and more productive for you and your child.

Problem	Solution
Is this a **problem?**	Work together on **solutions**.

Homework is too difficult.

Before he starts, make sure that he understands the concept and process. (Have him do the first few math problems with you.)

Ideally, assignments should be completed without help. If this does not seem possible, talk with the teacher; ask for suggestions.

Homework takes too long.

Talk with the teacher:
- Ask how much time he should spend (a primary non-LD student usually spends 20-30 minutes).
- Decide together on a time that the LD student should spend.
- Ask the teacher to reduce amount of work to be done (fewer math problems, shorter essay).
- Allow modifications (word processor, dictated assignments).

Lack of organization.

Provide a notebook with dividers, and folders for each subject, a zippered bag for pencils, pens, and supplies. (Put his name on everything.)

See our workpage,
which follows

Give the student an assignment book or a **daily home-work sheet** which can be initialled if written correctly. (This is hard to implement. Stick with it; it works!)

See our workpage,
which follows

Have the student make a **weekly schedule** (younger ones may need help). (1) List **all** after-school activities for the week (don't forget phone calls, meals, snacks, play-time, sports, homework). (2) Select a half hour to be used for planning the week. (3) Record everything. Make sure that long assignments are divided among days.

Leave books, notebooks, and other items needed for school in the same place each night. (Next to the door is best; never wait until the next morning.)

Unpleasant scenes at home.

Decide on the best time to complete homework (after school, after free time, after supper).

Provide a quiet work place (away from TV, conversation).

Decide who should give assistance (parent, grandparent, older sibling, neighbor, tutor).

Provide incentives ("When you have finished your homework, you may watch TV").

Set a kitchen timer and decide together how long he will work. Don't require perfection (errors explain to the teacher that the skill needs more work at school). Don't do it for him!

Praise for a job well done!

Daily Homework Sheet

Name _____   Date _____

Class/Subject	Assignment	Assignment Recorded Correctly (Teacher Initials)	Turned In (Teacher Initials)

Weekly Schedule

From _____ to _____
(dates)

Time	Sunday	Monday	Tuesday	Wednesday	Thursday	Friday	Saturday

Launching Better Behavior:

Accentuate The Positive[1]

Instructions

Read through the descriptions below. Put a check mark next to the items which best describe how you discipline your child and handle bad behavior.

Overall, are the techniques you are presently using positive techniques which will "launch your child to better behavior" or are they negative techniques?

Choose one or two areas in which you are presently using negative techniques and make a concerted effort in the next week to use the positive techniques

described. If necessary, jot yourself a reminder on "post-it" sticky notes and place on the refrigerator door or elsewhere to help you remember.

At the end of the week, review your progress and choose additional positive techniques to try.

[1]The suggestions which follow have been adapted from the following material: Guhse, M. *Behavior management tips.* A paper developed for Weekday Early Education, Richmond, VA.

Try this. . .	. . . instead of this
___ Use eye contact; speak directly to your child while he's looking at you	___ Call from across the room
___ Speak in short, meaningful sentences	___ Use a lot of words
___ Use positive instructions ("Speak softly, please.")	___ Use negative instructions ("Don't yell!")
___ Give one direction at a time	___ Expect too many things at once
___ Praise the behaviors you want to continue	___ Always emphasize negative behaviors
___ Praise the specific job ("That was a great job of setting the table.")	___ Just say "Good!"
___ Be specific when speaking about an undesirable behavior	___ Attack his personality or make him feel guilty
___ Make sure that your child knows the rules (Keep them simple and consistent. Ask him to repeat them.)	___ Deal with a situation only after it has happened
___ Use incentives ("When you have finished cleaning up your room, you may go outside to play.")	___ Make demands ("Clean up your room right this minute!")
___ Give choices when possible	___ Make all the decisions
___ Let your child know what to expect ("After you have played outside for a half hour, it will be time to do homework.") (LD children have trouble with time concepts; warn him when his play time is almost over.)	___ Surprise him ("Come in here this minute and do your homework!")
___ Follow through with what you say	___ Make empty promises or threats without acting
___ Model appropriate behavior	___ Do one thing yourself but expect something else from your child
___ Let the punishment fit the crime	___ Impose a major punishment for something minor
___ Remain calm when managing behavior	___ Become angry
___ Try a little laughter (Remember your sense of humor.)	___ Take life too seriously all the time

Which ones did you do? Try the positive ones in the left column. They work!

13 Parent Rules For
Responding To Angry Children[1]

Instructions

LD children are often angry at themselves, at you, and at school, and are stirred up inside. They may act out. It should be our goal not to make them ashamed or guilty for their anger, but to channel and redirect it to constructive uses. The "13 Parent Rules" are reminders. Place this poster in a readily visible place where you can check your responses.

- **Catch the child being good** (praise, praise, praise)

- **Ignore inappropriate behavior—unless it is dangerous**

- **Provide physical outlets to get rid of energy** (swimming, gymnastics, etc.)

- **Use closeness and touching** (your hand and touch are calming)

- **Show affection**

- **Ease tension through humor**

- **Explain situations**

- **Remove tough situations; control the environment**

- **Use** (and keep!) **promises; use rewards**

- **Say no!, but use punishment cautiously**

- **Model appropriate behavior** (children learn what they see)

- **Don't criticize or compare behavior** (brothers and sisters aren't perfect either)

- **Avoid Danger Words and Statements!**
  -Don't be stupid!
  -Your brother never did that!
  -When are you going to grow up!
  -I can't trust you!
  -Stop acting that way!
  -Can't you do anything right!
  -You're a mess!
  -How many times do I have to tell you!

AT THE END
OF YOUR ROPE?

[1]The above has been adapted from the following material: U.S. Department of Health, Education and Welfare. (1978) *Plain talk about dealing with an angry child.* Washington, DC: Author.

IV. The LD Student At School

School's Role - Identification And The Placement Process

As you might suspect, learning disabled children need special consideration at school as well as at home. If your child has not yet been identified as learning disabled, you may want the public school system to look into the situation. If so, you will need to contact your child's classroom teacher and school principal or counselor, or the special education coordinator (or supervisor) for your school division and request that your child be considered for special education services.

It is best to put this in writing, date your request, and keep a copy of it for your files, as this request is now a legal referral. You will see later in this chapter that upon receipt of your letter, the school is responsible for following time lines that are established by regulations in your state. (Figure 1)

The special education process, as mandated by federal and state law, is outlined on the following pages. The United States Congress passed Public Law 94-142 in November, 1975. Pursuant to that statute, as amended by Public Law 101–476 (Individuals with Disabilities Education Act—IDEA), the U.S. Department of Education established detailed regulations in regard to the identification and education of handicapped children. The key provisions and protections provided by federal law are summarized in Appendix E.

Should you wish to refer to the law itself, you will find the federal statute in Volume 20 of the United States Code in Sections 1400 through 1485 and the legal "citation" is 20 U.S.C. Section 1400–1485. The federal regulations are located in Volume 34 of the Code of Federal Regulations, Part 300 and are cited as 34 CFR Part 300. Most law libraries will have the United States Code (USC) and the Code of Federal Regulations (CFR).

In response to the federal law, each state has also issued its own regulations which provide detailed timelines and procedures. It is important that you secure from your State Department of Education a copy of the actual regulations. That agency will probably also have a booklet or packet of information that is less technical and provides an explanation of the state regulations. All states also have another agency usually known as the Department of Rights for the Disabled or the Protection and Advocacy Office. You should also contact them for all literature, pamphlets and booklets they have about the state regulations and you and your child's rights. (*See* Appendix C)

By becoming familiar with your state's timelines and descriptive labels for meetings, etc. you will appear and be more self assured and confident.

If your local school system has adopted its own guidelines and regulations, they must be consistent with the regulations published by your State Department of Education and those "regs" in turn must be consistent with the federal regulations. Once you have your state regs and other state and local publications about the special education procedural process, you should know and fill in the timelines on page 42, entitled "The Special Education Process." If the names of the committees differ, you will be familiar with your state's "jargon." Also provided, in the glossary, are descriptions of the committees referred to below.

Referral

The referral process for a student who is suspected of having a learning disability usually begins by having the youngster referred to the principal, guidance counselor, or special education coordinator. This referral can be made by a parent, teacher, school counselor, or other school personnel; even the student can make the referral.

The Special Education Process

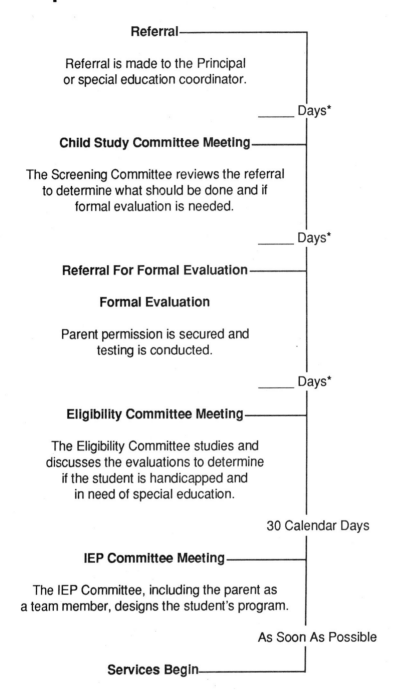

Referral

Referral is made to the Principal
or special education coordinator.

_____ Days*

Child Study Committee Meeting

The Screening Committee reviews the referral
to determine what should be done and if
formal evaluation is needed.

_____ Days*

Referral For Formal Evaluation

Formal Evaluation

Parent permission is secured and
testing is conducted.

_____ Days*

Eligibility Committee Meeting

The Eligibility Committee studies and
discusses the evaluations to determine
if the student is handicapped and
in need of special education.

30 Calendar Days

IEP Committee Meeting

The IEP Committee, including the parent as
a team member, designs the student's program.

As Soon As Possible

Services Begin

Parent permission is secured and
special education begins.

*NOTE: Each state may have slightly different timeframes within which the school system must respond. Contact
your state's Department of Education (_see_ Appendix C) to determine the time allocated for each step in this process
in your state and then complete this chart with the appropriate number of days for your state.

Figure 1

Child Study Committee Meeting

Once the school has received the referral, the school's Child Study Committee (the name may be different in your state) must review the referral information within the designated number of days to decide if formal evaluation is needed. The committee studies test scores, teacher reports, information that you as a parent have provided, teaching techniques which have been used, and other information related to your child's current problems.

After reviewing all this information, the committee may recommend further consultations with a specialist, the classroom teacher or teachers, or persons outside of the school system who may be working with your child. The committee may recommend that the classroom teacher try some strategies that haven't been used before; sometimes this can eliminate the necessity for comprehensive testing or moving your youngster into special education. Or the committee may recommend a formal evaluation. Sometimes other evaluations may be requested to determine needs in areas such as audiology, physical therapy, occupational therapy, or speech and language. You as a parent may request, in writing, a report of the outcome of the Child Study Committee's deliberations.

If this committee decides not to refer your child for formal evaluation, it must provide a date on which to review the results of the alternate recommendations it has made. Be certain that any alternate strategies are clearly specified so that they can be properly monitored.

Reasons for Disagreements Among Professionals

Now is probably the time in this guide to bring up a subject that may affect you and your child: the fact that many professionals can disagree on who is and is not learning disabled. What is difficult for even many people in the field of education to comprehend is that there is not one set of people who **are** LD and another set of people who **are not** LD. We almost all have learning difficulties in some aspect of our lives. Some people who are exceptionally skilled with language and who may, in fact, become English teachers are not able to keep their checkbooks straight. There are other people who become nuclear physicists who never do learn to spell correctly. There is also a huge group who never failed a subject in school but who are at a complete loss when it comes to figuring out a schematic or a diagram for making simple house repairs or assembling toys.

These individual learning difficulties may appear to be similar to characteristics often used to describe a person with learning disabilities. However, it is when an individual's learning difficulties are so pervasive, so severe that they markedly interfere with day-to-day living that the person may be suspected of being LD.

The following groups of children with LD characteristics frequently become the focus of hot debate among professionals trying to determine if they need special education help: those who are at the low-average end of the IQ scale, those who are highly intelligent, and those whose social and economic experiences have been unusual when compared with their peers.

School people may disagree, when looking at the records of a low-average IQ student, concerning the reason for the academic difficulties. Some may claim that the lower intelligence is the basis of the problem, while others may feel strongly that if it weren't for the learning disability, the youngster could do better academically or at least make passing grades.

On the other hand, a learning disabled student with a high-average or superior IQ may have compensated quite satisfactorily for the problems faced in the lower grades, but may be unable to manage in the higher grades when faced with taking lecture notes, preparing longer reading assignments, and perhaps completing a foreign language requirement. Some professionals are baffled by such a student and claim that since the youngster didn't appear to have academic problems earlier, there's no reason to entertain the possibility that a learning disability is the reason for the onset of the current problems.

Then there's that third group of LD students who have had a less-than-conventional upbringing. They may have lived in a number of different foster homes, or been malnourished, abused, or have attended six different schools in two years. Some professionals will feel that there is no learning disability—that the academic problems stem from the social and/or economic background. However, the clue concerning the presence or absence of a specific learning disability lies in the characteristics of the youngster under consideration. A child **can** be learning disabled and at the same time come from a non-traditional background.

Each of these situations can provide the basis for sincere disagreement among caring and well-intentioned professionals on the Child Study Committee or on the Eligibility Committee. In such circumstances, it is particularly important for parents to be well informed about learning disabilities and to provide the groups of professionals with as much well-considered information about their youngster as possible.

Formal Assessment Begun

If the Child Study Committee determines that your child needs formal evaluation, its recommendation that the testing be done must be made to the Special Education Administrator within the designated number of days in your state. The Child Study Committee is required to document its decision in writing, including the information upon which its recommendation for testing was based. Again, you as the parent are entitled to request and review this report. However, before formal evaluation can be started, the school division must have your written permission.

A complete and individual evaluation is made in the following areas: educational, medical (including vision and hearing screening), sociocultural, and psychological (and others if needed). In addition, students suspected of being learning disabled must be observed in their classrooms by someone other than the regular teacher. These components comprise a "comprehensive evaluation."

A general description of each component follows:

Educational

An educational evaluation, which may be made by the LD teacher, is submitted in a written report. The evaluation may include, but is not limited to, assessment of present levels of achievement in basic academic skill areas such as reading, written expression (spelling, penmanship, composition), and mathematics. It may also assess functioning in basic psychological processes such as visual-motor performance, concept formation, memory, auditory perception, fine and gross motor development, and psycholinguistic processes.

Educational assessment should not be based solely upon grades, report cards, or the results of a single test, but on data gathered through use of a battery of tests and teachers' reports. These may be a combination of standardized, teacher-made, and/or criterion referenced tests. Diagnostic teaching procedures may also be used. If standardized tests are used, the test scores are included in the educational report.

In addition to the diagnostic data described above, the following information is relevant for the Eligibility Committee to consider:

1. History of educational experiences including age at which student entered first grade, attendance, grades repeated, and letter/ number grades earned;

2. Description of current class performance and work habits;
3. Description of student's strengths;
4. Description of peer and adult relationships;
5. Description of successful and unsuccessful interventions tried previously;
6. Description of specific educational needs which cannot be met in general education alone.

Much of this latter information can be obtained from a representative of the Child Study Committee and the student's confidential file. If not, every effort should be made to obtain this information during the assessment process.

(Note: The Glossary provides a detailed listing and explanation of educational tests.)

Medical

The medical evaluation should identify any physiological factors which might interfere with the learning process. A medical and developmental history should be obtained, with note made of any condition or current drug regimen which might affect classroom performance. Although gross vision and hearing screening may have revealed no major problems, subtle difficulties may be caught with more comprehensive testing. For example, impedance screening, a more sophisticated hearing assessment, may be indicated.

Socio-Cultural

Relevant factors in the social history which might support the need for LD services are: history of developmental lag, familial learning problems, and evidence that the learning problems are not due **primarily** to environmental, cultural or economic disadvantage. Such information may be obtained by a school social worker or a visiting teacher through the use of interview techniques and social behavior checklists.

Psychological

A psychological evaluation performed by a psychologist shall include individual tests of intellectual functioning, affective behavior and personality assessments as needed, and other psychological tests as appropriate.

Group intelligence test scores will not give appropriate information for LD students, as these tests rely upon reading skill—which may be affected by the LD student's handicap.

The written report should include a statement of intellectual potential, verbal and performance scores, and scaled subtest scores (when the test used yields such scores), as well as interpretation of this information. Such assessment data is not only germane to eligibility procedures, but also highly relevant to the development of the Individualized Education Program (IEP).

Observation

The federal regulations requiring observation of the student who is suspected of being learning disabled read as follows:

> At least one team member other than the child's regular teacher shall observe the child's academic performance in the regular classroom setting. In the case of a child of less than school age, or out of school, a team member shall observe the child in an environment appropriate for a child of that age.

The results of the observation are presented in a written report which includes data on the length of the observation, the behavior noted during the observation which is relevant to a diagnosis of learning disabilities, and the relationship of that behavior to the student's academic functioning.

Other

When indicated, assessment of speech, language, motor abilities, etc., should also be made. If a student is determined to need the services of a speech/language pathologist, a physical therapist, counselor, or special arrangements for bus service, etc., these are considered **Related Services**, and must be included in the IEP.

Eligibility Committee Meeting

Generally, within a certain number of days of the decision by the Child Study Committee that formal evaluation is needed, all five parts of the comprehensive evaluation must be completed, and the Eligibility Committee must meet to study and discuss the evaluations in order to determine if your child is to be classified as handicapped and in need of special education and/or related services. (It is important that, as a parent, you recognize that this is the terminology that is used in the laws. The public school is required to provide special services **only** after your child is deemed "handicapped and in need of special education and/or related services.")

After the evaluation process has been completed, you, the parent, have a right to review the information,

to obtain copies of the evaluation, and to request that the evaluations be explained to you. You may also request that you be allowed to attend the Eligibility Committee meeting.

IEP Committee Meeting

If it has been determined that your child is in need of special education, an Individualized Education Program (IEP) Committee meeting must be held within 30 **calendar** days of that determination to outline a program for your child for the school year, based on the youngster's individual needs. It must be developed **after** your child is determined in need of special education services and **before** services begin.

Not only must you, as parent, be involved in the preparation of the IEP, but you must also approve the placement before services are begun. If you cannot attend the IEP meeting, you must, upon your request, be provided a full and complete report of the meeting.

It bears repeating that the laws and regulations do assure parents the right to participate in the development of the IEP. This right represents an opportunity **and** a responsibility whereby parents can provide input to their child's educational program. It important that parents understand fully what is being discussed. If necessary parents should request additional time and clarification.

Although different school systems may use different forms, the law requires that the following information be included in every IEP:

- The present levels of educational performance: Up-to-date information documenting test results in basic academic, vocational and/or social skills; should include test names, dates administered and test results; data should be included on any area which has been identified as a weakness for your child.

- Specific educational services: Statement of **all** services which the child is to receive, including the type of special education program, i.e., LD; particular model of service delivery (see pp. 48–49); number of hours per day in special education; number of hours per day in regular education; accommodations, e.g., oral testing, taped textbooks, etc., to be made in the regular classroom; related services, e.g., counseling, physical therapy, etc.

● Projected date for initiation and anticipated duration of services: Dates indicate when services will begin and end.

● Annual goals and short-term instructional objectives: Goal statements indicating the general intent and direction of the services provided on a yearly basis. Goal statements should be included for every area of weakness indicated by tests and/or observation and documented under "present levels of educational performance;" short-term instructional objectives should be included for each goal and should map out a systematic sequence of skills needed to achieve the goal.

● Appropriate objective criteria and evaluation procedures: Statements included in each goal and objective identifying the level or degree of mastery required and how it will be tested, i.e., "How will we know that the student has learned this?"

● Date and method of annual review: IEP committee must meet at least once each school year to evaluate the IEP, student progress, and whether the instructional objectives are being met.

For secondary students only:

● Statement as to whether student is working towards graduation with a diploma and what accommodations, if any, are needed. Some states and school systems make a distinction, at the completion of high school, in awarding some handicapped students a "certificate of attendance," which signifies completion of four years' attendance, rather than graduation from high school. Therefore, IEPs for secondary level LD students should clearly state whether the individual is working towards a certificate of attendance or a diploma, i.e., graduation. Accommodations which may be needed on any state or

school mandated testing program, as a prerequisite to graduation, should also be included.

● Statement as to what transition services are planned for the student's move from school to the post-school environment. This may include plans for accessing post-secondary education, vocational training and so forth and should include a list of any agencies, in addition to the school, responsible for services.

(*See* Appendix D for an example of a blank IEP.)

Parents should carefully review the IEP. Do not sign the IEP until you have studied it thoroughly and understand it. You should be aware that you have the right to have someone (another parent or professional) accompany you to the IEP meeting. You may also take home your copy of the IEP before signing it and consult with other professionals and knowledgeable parents. You may wish to contact a local parent group, Parent Information and Training Center or representative from your state Protection and Advocacy agency, if you have questions or concerns (*see* Appendix C).

Once you sign the IEP, you are, in effect, giving permission for your child to receive the services designated. The school division must base the placement of your child on the IEP. It is required to provide **only** those services **specifically** stated in the IEP, so you must be sure they are included if they are needed. Parents should be aware that school divisions are not required to provide the **best** program for a student, only an **appropriate** program.

A well-written IEP is the tool by which parents and teachers develop and monitor a student's program and progress. If you have concerns that the program is not meeting your child's needs, you may request that the IEP committee be reconvened to review the IEP.

School's Role—The LD Program

Parents sometimes feel that simply by having their child tested and diagnosed as learning disabled, their problems will be solved. Identification and diagnosis, however, are really just the first step. Once a child has been identified as learning disabled, it is then necessary to begin planning an educational program and to determine what services will be needed to succeed in school. It is important for parents to understand those educational services and programs available for the learning disabled so that they can communicate effectively with the professionals working with their child.

Organizational Models

The development of the IEP is the process by which this planning takes place (*see* pages 45–46 and Appendix D). Since each child's strengths and weaknesses and learning needs are unique, this is a very individualized process. If you were to study the IEPs of several learning disabled children, chances are that each one would be different, reflecting the different needs of each student.

The IEP process notwithstanding, schools must organize the various services they provide for all learning disabled students into different service delivery models, i.e., they must determine how they will provide different types of services, grouping them into programs and classes. According to federal and state law, every public school system must provide a continuum of services. That is, school systems must have services or programs in which only minimal special help is available for students with mild learning disabilities, programs where intensive special help is provided for students with severe handicaps, as well as alternatives which fall between these extremes. It is in this context that you will hear mentioned terms such as "least restrictive environment" (LRE) and "mainstreaming." Federal and state laws require that the severity of a child's learning disability be considered when placing a student in a particular setting. Students with mild to moderate disabilities will be placed in less restrictive settings, while students with severe disabilities may be placed in more restrictive settings. In special education, the notion of "restrictiveness" generally applies to the extent to which the LD student is integrated or segregated from a regular classroom setting with nonhandicapped peers (*See* Figure 2, which follows). When an LD student receives all or a portion of his instruction within a regular classroom, this is known as "mainstreaming." Mainstreaming is neither inherently "good" nor "bad." The extent to which an LD child can be mainstreamed successfully will depend upon a variety of factors, including the **severity of the disability**, as well as the **willingness and flexibility of the regular classroom teacher in modifying the curriculum** to meet the needs of the child. And so, just as IEPs will differ from LD child to LD child, so will the notion of LRE for learning disabled students.

It may help you to visualize this continuum of possible service delivery models if it is depicted as a pyramid of services. (*See* following page.)

Pyramid of Services[1]

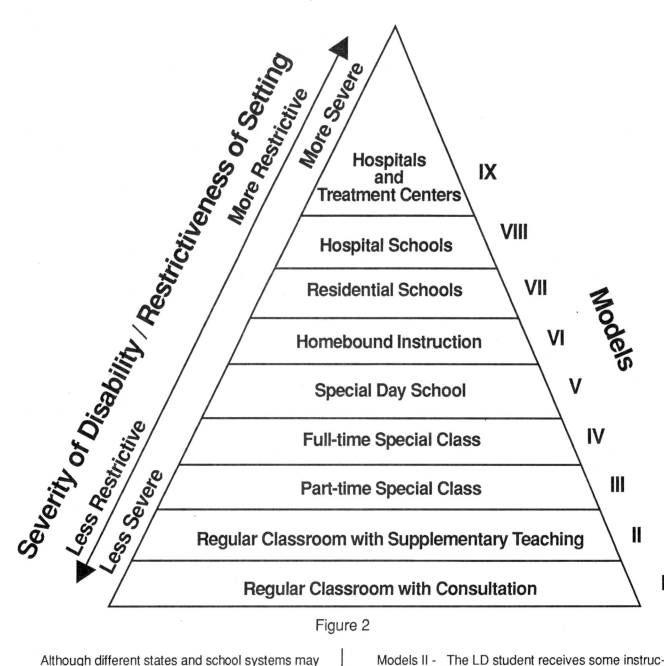

Figure 2

Although different states and school systems may have different names for the programs they provide for LD students, most services fall within the general structure depicted by the pyramid diagram:

Model I- In this model, frequently called a "consultation model," the LD student continues to receive all instruction in a regular classroom. The LD teacher consults with the classroom teacher on a regular basis, monitoring the student's progress, making suggestions as to how to adapt materials and assignments, etc.

Models II- The LD student receives some instruc-
& III tion from a regular classroom teacher and some from a trained LD teacher; the exact proportion of time spent with each teacher will depend upon the child's needs. Team teaching, with the LD teacher working with the student and classroom teacher within the context of the regular classroom, is a possible example of Model II. Model III is most often called a "resource room" model, whereby the LD child is pulled out of the regular classroom for a certain period of time in order to work

with the LD teacher, usually in a small group setting, in a separate room. In order for these models to be successful, the regular classroom and LD teachers must work closely together to coordinate instruction.

Model IV -   Frequently referred to as a "self-contained classroom," this model is one in which all the children in the class have disabilities; the number of children in the class is generally much smaller than that in a regular classroom. The children receive most of their instruction in this class from an LD teacher. However, because the class is housed in a regular school, students still have an opportunity to interact with nonhandicapped peers in extracurricular activities.

Model V -   Although some public school systems do have special schools devoted entirely to the education of learning disabled students, it is more common to find this model in private schools.

Model VI -   In general, homebound instruction for an LD student would be a temporary measure if, for some reason, the student were unable to attend school for a relatively short period of time (e.g., severe asthma, a broken leg, etc.).

Model VII -   Residential schools for LD students offer a 24-hour environment in which the student attends school and lives with other LD students for a part of the year.

Models VIII - and IX   These models are the most restrictive settings for a student. In general, they would be chosen only if a child had severe medical and/or emotional problems, as well as learning disabilities.

It is important for parents to remember that federal and state laws mandate that public school systems provide a continuum of services. If a school system does not have certain levels of service within its own system and if it is determined that your LD child needs this level of service, then the school system must seek the needed services outside of the system and must pay any tuition and transportation costs.

Remedial Approaches

At some point, you may find yourself asking one of the following questions:

How is the LD classroom different from the regular classroom in which my LD child has been so frustrated?

What does the LD teacher do that is so different from what the regular classroom teacher does?

If you were to observe in an LD class, you would discover that the instructional techniques used by the LD teacher are neither magical nor mysterious. The strategies are simply good teaching techniques, applied in a consistent manner in a small class setting.

While not all LD teachers or classes are the same, were you to observe, you would very likely note the following features in an LD class:

● Low teacher-pupil ratio: Instruction is usually provided in small groups and sometimes on a 1-1 basis.

● Individualized instruction: The scope and sequence of the instruction presented to a particular student is based on an assessment of the student's skills and is not determined simply by the contents of the textbook. Therefore, the teacher does not automatically start at page one of the textbook and proceed through it, page by page; the teacher matches the instruction and materials to the student's needs.

● Use of task analysis: Concepts and skills are analyzed by the teacher and then broken down and taught in small, incremental steps, one step building upon the other.

● Acknowledgement of learning style: The teacher recognizes that students learn differently (some by doing, some by example, etc.) and tries to match the **instructional** style to the student's particular **learning** style.

- "Success philosophy": This philosophy is intertwined with the individualization of instruction, task analysis and acknowledgement of learning style. By presenting instruction on the student's level, in small steps, and in a way that capitalizes upon the student's learning style, the teacher tries to insure that the student is successful at learning.

- High degree of structure and organization: Student expectations are clearly stated so that students know what is required, what will happen next, etc. The classroom environment may also be highly structured with tables or desks arranged to designate certain activities and areas of study.

- Availability of a variety of instructional materials and approaches: While teachers in the regular classroom may use only one particular reading series or approach, the LD teacher may have a variety of materials or approaches from which to choose, and often incorporates several materials and approaches in teaching any given skill.

- Multisensory approach to learning: While there are many possible instructional approaches, a multisensory approach involving as many senses as possible seems to be effective for many LD children. It is often called the VAKT approach (Visual-Auditory-Kinesthetic-Tactile). An example is the child who practices his spelling words by looking at the word while simultaneously saying the names of the letters and tracing the letters in a sand tray.

- Slower pace of instruction and frequent repetition: Concepts and skills are presented and practiced over and over again in a variety of ways to insure that the student "overlearns" and truly masters them.

- Instruction in coping strategies: Students are taught ways to "work around" their specific learning disabilities; for example, they may learn strategies for improving memory, focusing attention, completing an assignment, etc.

- Close monitoring of student progress: A "test-teach-retest" approach may be used to determine what skills a student lacks and whether he has mastered them, following instruction. This is an ongoing process.

- Use of a motivational system: Principles of behavior modification are used to motivate and reward students to work to the best of their abilities. Points and contract systems are frequently used.

- Direct instruction in social skills. Some LD students need direct help in relating to other people effectively.

Accommodation vs. Remediation

While it is difficult, and even unwise, to make generalizations about educational programming for all LD students, professionals usually agree that, in order to be successful in both the long and short term, educational programs for the learning disabled must include a balance of both "accommodation" and "remediation."

- **Accommodation** is the modification and adaptation of materials (textbooks, workbooks, worksheets, etc.), assignments, class requirements, etc. so that the LD student is able to work around or bypass his specific disabilities and still participate in and benefit from classroom activities. Examples of accommodations include tape-recording textbook material so that a student with a reading disability may listen to the material; permitting a student who has difficulty expressing his thoughts in writing to make oral, instead of written, presentations (such as book reports); allotting additional time for the completion of tests, etc.

- **Remediation** is the improvement in specific skills through individualized instruction. For example, a student whose learning disability manifests itself as inability or difficulty in reading might receive specific instruction in those reading skills which have not yet been mastered.

As noted above, a balanced LD program will include both accommodation and remediation. For the student who has just begun to receive LD assistance or for the student with a severe learning disability, accommodations in the regular classroom are especially critical. While the student may be working with the LD teacher to remediate basic deficits, it does take time to build these skills. In the meantime, then, it is important to minimize the student's lack of success and frustration in the regular classroom by making modifications and accommodations, so that the youngster is not penalized for the learning disability.

Likewise, it is not sufficient to just modify the LD student's classroom environment in order to accommodate the existing disabilities. This sometimes occurs at the secondary level where LD teachers often go to great lengths to encourage regular classroom teachers to allow students to take tests orally, give oral reports, have shorter assignments, etc. This may be necessary for the student's immediate, short term success; however, it must be supplemented by remediation of the basic skills (reading, spelling, composition, etc.) which necessitated the accommodations in the first place. Only then is long term success possible, going beyond just making a passing grade in a particular class. Graduation, with a successful, fulfilling life beyond school is the goal. The LD instruction may provide the last chance the student has to learn basic skills. Once the student has graduated, the opportunities to gain these skills are very limited.

It may be important to note here that, despite remediation in school, many LD individuals will need accommodations as adults, whether in the context of their job, day-to-day living, or social relations. Learning disabilities are never really "cured." However, it is appropriate to expect that, with the proper help in school, learning disabled young adults will assume increasing responsibility for devising their own accommodations and solutions to daily obstacles.

The "Right" Program

Once your child has been identified as learning disabled, you as a parent may find yourself in a never-ending search for the "right" LD program. You may find yourself wondering how you will ever find the "right" program. It may help to keep in mind the information presented in the previous sections on educational services, as well as the following important points:

- There is no "right" program for all LD students. Programs are "right" or appropriate for each child only to the extent to which the instruction and services provided address the identified needs and deficits of the student.

- Each student's IEP really represents that individual's "program." A resource room or self-contained class is not a program; they are just the organizational structures used to deliver services.

- The goals and objectives of the student's IEP should be identified first; then (and only then) the service delivery model in which these objectives can most appropriately be met should be identified.

- A student's program/IEP should be developed on the basis of what the student needs, not what services are presently available in the school system. Beware of any LD teacher or administrator who tells you, "What your child really needs is _____, but we don't have that available." The intent of the law is that school systems must either provide the most appropriate service or provide the funds needed to secure it elsewhere.

- Examine the papers which your child brings home from the LD class. Determine whether the work reflected in the papers correlates with the goals and objectives of the IEP. For example, if testing has revealed deficits in reading comprehension and subsequent goals for the improvement of reading comprehension were included on the IEP, then classwork should reflect this focus. If you do not find a correlation between IEP objectives and classwork, request a meeting with the teacher and/or IEP committee to clarify the situation.

- Monitor your student's progress carefully. Ask for frequent feedback. If your child is not making progress in the LD class, request an IEP meeting to consider possible revisions. If your child is making progress in the LD class but not in the mainstream, meet with teachers to ascertain whether additional accommodations within the regular classrooms are possible or whether additional time is needed in the LD class. Remember to balance accommodation and remediation.

- Be aware that, sometimes, students with other handicapping conditions (emotional disturbance, mental retardation, etc.) may be placed in special classes with LD students. This is most likely to happen in smaller school systems. Such a classroom situation places great demands upon the teacher. If your child is in such a setting, be especially careful to monitor progress to be certain that your youngster's needs are being met.

- A special note to parents of high school students: Keep in mind that in order to graduate from high school with a diploma, some state laws may mandate that students must meet certain requirements, such as acquiring the required number of Carnegie units (credits awarded for classes), passing certain "competency" tests, etc. Early in the high school program, parents, teachers and the student should discuss whether the student will attempt to meet these requirements in order to obtain a diploma. This decision will influence (and will be influenced by) the type of LD program in which the student participates. For example, a student who receives much daily instruction from the LD teacher may be unable to earn a sufficient number of Carnegie units for a diploma. The IEP Committee is responsible for documenting the decision made.

Suspension and Expulsion of LD Students

Unfortunate as it may be, some LD students find themselves faced with the possibility of suspension or expulsion as a result of some type of unacceptable behavior. Where a disciplinary action involves long-term suspension (more than ten days) or expulsion of an LD student, a determination must be made as to whether or not there is a direct causal relationship between the nature of the learning disability and the misconduct. If a direct causal relation is found, suspension or expulsion must be considered a change in placement and thus the child's IEP committee must meet to assess the appropriateness of the child's current placement. Therefore, documentation of any behavioral disorders related to the learning disability should be noted at the initial development of the IEP.

Parents should contact the individual responsible for supervising the special education programs in their school to request a copy of school policy with regard to suspension (in and out of school) and expulsion. Some school systems view the accumulation of ten nonconsecutive days of suspension during a school year as a change of placement also and again would require that the IEP committee reconvene to assess the appropriateness of the current placement.

As a result of the landmark case, *Honig* v. *Doe*, 484 U.S. 305, 108 S. Ct. 52, 98 L. Ed 2d.686 (1988) most states have enacted regulations for dealing with suspension and expulsion of handicapped students. Should your youngster be faced with either of these possibilities, contact your state's Department of Education or Protection and Advocacy Agency to determine your child's specific rights in your state. (*See* Appendix C).

Relationship of Public and Private Services

Students in private schools can avail themselves of special education services at no cost. If your child is enrolled in a private school and you suspect a learning disability, and if you wish to determine eligibility for special education and related services at your local public school, contact the individual responsible for supervising the special education programs within your school system.

You should make a written referral stating your concern and requesting a formal evaluation of your child by the public schools to determine eligibility for special education and related services. According to federal and state law, your child, while attending a private school, is entitled to this evaluation at no charge by the public schools.

Once the child has been evaluated, eligibility proceedings take place as described on page 45. If your child is found to be learning disabled, the public school system is required to offer appropriate services, programs, and placement consistent with your child's IEP.

As a parent, you may choose to accept the services offered by the public schools or you may choose to continue your child in private school placement. Should you choose to continue the private school placement, so long as an appropriate education is available, the public school system is **not** obligated to pay for your child's education at the private school. However, the public school **is** required to provide special education and related services to meet your youngster's unique needs. Such services may be provided through arrangements such as dual enrollment, educational television, and the use of mobile educational services and equipment. The public school system may provide services to private school children which differ from those provided for children actually attending the public school if the differences are necessary to meet the special needs of the private school children and if the services are comparable in quality, scope, and opportunity for participation with those provided to students in public schools. The local school system maintains administrative control of these services, as governed by the IEP.

There are private testing agencies which parents may decide to use. However, you should recognize, if this is your choice, that the schools are required only to **consider** this information, along with the other information they have accumulated. As was pointed out earlier in this chapter, disagreements do arise among professionals; those operating from private testing agencies will not necessarily agree with the conclusions arrived at by the professionals operating within the public schools.

Parents who have been dealing with private schools and agencies should be aware that their child will enter the process described in this chapter at the point of the Eligibility Committee.

[1]Reynolds, M. (1962). A framework for considering some issues in special education. *Exceptional Children,* March, 1962, p. 368.

Parents' Role

It is important for all parents to be concerned with their child's educational program; but as a parent of a learning disabled child, your involvement is essential if your child is to be provided the best possible educational experiences. In trying to assure the best possible experience, you will want to present yourself in a positive and assertive fashion.[1]

Never forget that parents have primary responsibility for their children's well-being. This means that you are an equal member of the decision-making team for your child's education. Your role as an evaluator of your child's program is very important, and your behavior and manner when meeting with educators will give an indication to the school of the degree of your interest and expertise in this role.[2]

At the outset, parents should do everything possible to avoid problems. While the law stipulates that you should be involved in decision-making activities because you know your child better than anyone else, it is important to interact in a positive manner with the people who work with your child.[3] Of great help in maintaining a positive and cooperative but assertive attitude is the knowledge that you have at hand a complete written record of your child's development, educational history, and a file of all correspondence, phone calls, and meetings pertaining to his or her education. (*See* pp. 55–57 for suggestions on compiling such information.) It is also important to become thoroughly acquainted with the key provisions of the federal and state laws and regulations that affect the education of children with special needs. (*See* Appendix E for a complete description of parental rights as mandated by law.) But passing laws doesn't guarantee your child will receive educational services as intended. People make it happen. Knowing how to assert your rights appropriately is more effective in gaining a better educational program for your child. If parent-school disagreements do arise, these same laws stipulate specific processes for resolution.[4] (*See* pp. 57–58 and Appendices E and F for Due Process

information.) Among the resources available to you is your state's Protection and Advocacy agency. It can help resolve disputes even prior to instigating due process procedures. (*See* Appendix C.)

Avoiding Problems

Until your child becomes mature enough to become his or her own advocate, you, the parent, must assume that role. You play a vital part in shaping your child's school experiences; therefore, you should begin preparations early in your youngster's school career.

One of the first things you can do is to join your school's PTA and attend as many meetings as possible. In this way you will get to know the principal and the teachers in a non-threatening setting. If possible, volunteer to be a room parent, or to accompany your child's class on field trips, so that you can form positive relationships, and the problems that may arise do not constitute your only involvement with the school.

Read about other children with problems similar to those of your child. Learn as much as you can about the ways in which other parents have handled them. Gain an understanding of your child's strengths and weaknesses. Ask questions of any professionals who have worked with your child. They can help you to understand the professionals' interpretation of test scores, to understand the way in which your child learns, and to be aware of special services your child may require. Build your self-confidence through knowledge. Now you can approach the school with assurance. Be pleasant and let your attitude reflect your desire to make positive contributions to the decisions being made for your child's education.

Try to build a good working relationship with your child's teacher and any of the other professionals who demonstrate empathy and understanding of your role as the principal monitor and important decision-maker for your child. Most teachers are very dedicated and hard working. You should try to work with them, not against them, if at all possible. Making life miserable for your child's teacher is not a ticket to a better education for your child. The best path to a better education is joint decision-making, mutual respect and teamwork— with you as a vital member of that team.[5]

Participate in all meetings and activities concerning your child. When possible, both parents should participate. When appropriate, your child may also participate.

In communicating with the school, you should rely primarily on written notes or letters of which you keep a copy. Use telephone calls for only the least important issues. Your copy of your written communication is documentation for your files.

Prepare for meetings by making a list of issues beforehand in the order of importance. In this way those points of primary concern to you and your child will be discussed first. Do not feel inadequate in the presence of professionals because of their credentials. Remember, this is **your** child, and you have known this child longer and more intimately than anyone else on the team.[6] Insist—politely—that the results of testing and evaluation be explained to you in clear, jargon-free terms and that you have copies for your own file.[7] Ask questions so that you and the school have the same understanding of terms. Listen to the views of all participants. Many times the solution to a problem is the combination of several ingredients—some previously unknown to you. Be as clear as possible in your own mind about what kind of things you believe your child is ready to learn. Make sure that the others at the conference never forget that you're talking about a real child.

Take some time beforehand to think about how to be assertive without "taking over" or antagonizing people. Meetings about a child's school needs are not intended to be hostile confrontations; they should provide the chance for honest examination of alternatives. It should be possible to iron out disagreements through persuasion and mutual understanding.[8]

Express your concerns and ideas. From daily observation under all conditions, you can contribute much concerning your child's strengths and weak-

nesses. You may know that your child becomes particularly lethargic right after lunch or has particular difficulty in following directions when not sitting near the front of the room. At the same time, you may be able to point out strengths your child possesses that the school was not aware of, such as having the ability to redesign and construct bicycles or play a musical instrument, or having a wealth of knowledge about and appreciation of music. You may have ideas or questions that no one else has brought up. Don't be reluctant to ask questions or make contributions to the discussion.[9] Providing an outlet for a child's special interest or ability will help create a more balanced day and may prevent boredom or behavior problems. Success in something can be a great morale booster.

As the year progresses, check on the effectiveness of the program designed for your child. If you have doubts, again ask questions and participate actively in finding causes for any lack of progress and in making adjustments to the educational plan. Listen to your child; respect what he or she is saying. You need to know your youngster's reaction to schoolwork, to teachers, to classmates.[10] At the same time, be aware that there may be two sides to the picture. You need to keep an open mind to viewing **both** sides. It is useful for you to be able to state the other point of view, even if you do not accept it; in putting into words the view opposite to your own, you can be better assured that you thoroughly understand it.

If you assume that someone else will surely say or do something if your child's problems are serious, you may be sadly disappointed. It is the parent who has discovered the futility of this assumption and who moves past the pain, the guilt, and the anger who can help his child. It is okay to ask for help. It doesn't mean you are a bad parent. You waited because you didn't know what else to do. Now, go ahead. Ask for service. Ask for clarification. Ask for information. Seek the answers. Don't accept "wait and see."[11]

Keeping a File

Over the years of your LD child's development, you will accumulate a drawer full of notes, records, and documents. There will be birth and social security records, your diary of important developmental milestones (e.g., age when began to talk and walk), medical records, report cards, correspondence pertaining to your child's education, your notes of telephone conversations, notes of school meetings you've attended, psychological and educational test reports, photographs, fingerprint record, and samples of your child's school work. These records have great significance. It is important to safeguard them and keep them organized for quick reference. The purpose of this section of the workbook is to help you set up a file.

Keeping a file is time-consuming, but it is one of the most important things that parents of learning disabled children can do. Accurate and accessible records are needed at every step along the way—when your child enters a new school, is considered for special services, needs medical or mental health services, requires legal intervention in case of disagreement with the school system, or, in the post-school years, seeks rehabilitation, professional or career training services, or is the object of your estate planning. Furthermore, as a parent of a child diagnosed with a handicap, you may qualify for insurance and tax benefits for certain expenses. Claiming these will require reference to your file.

The suggestions that follow have come from parents, educators, and legal experts.

- Date each item in the lower right-hand corner in pencil. Do this even if the date appears elsewhere on the document. This date will be used to keep and to locate documents in chronological order. In case of documents which span a period of time, such as report cards and telephone logs, use date of the last entry.

- Maintain records in an oversized, 3-hole looseleaf notebook, whenever possible. Arrange records in chronological order, oldest document last, most recent first. Use this notebook to keep **all** records pertaining to your child's learning disability and educational progress. You will want to include the following:

  - Report Cards: Official school and interim report cards, as well as written comments from all teachers, camp counselors, Sunday School teachers, tutors, etc.

  - Correspondence: All correspondence received as well as copies of letters which you have written about your LD child.

  - Medical Test Reports: Significant birth and developmental history, visual exams, auditory evaluations, etc.

  - Psychological and Educational Test Reports: Also include any notes you made during interpretive conferences following these evaluations.

  - Telephone Log: This would include a record of significant telephone conversations with teachers and other professionals. Be sure to include the date, time, name of the person you talked with, the subject and substance of the conversation, and any follow-up steps to be taken.

  - Special Education Documentation: Referral, child study, eligibility, IEP, and all other official documents pertaining to your child's special education process and program.

- Never highlight or write on the documents (excepting date in lower right corner). If you wish to call attention to particular passages, affix "post-it" notes with your comments.

- Do keep a log of your telephone communications (*see above*).

- Do keep a written summary of each meeting you have with teachers and other professionals.

- Secure a complete and entire copy of your child's cumulative and confidential file from the school system and from all agencies that have ever evaluated or worked with your child. Familiarize yourself with these records and place them in the notebook in chronological order.

- Maintain a table of contents or chronological list of documents. Each document is entered according to date, author, description of type of document, and brief summary or explanation. If author is unknown or not available, use name of the agency or school system. It is helpful to store this chronological list of documents on a word processor, if one is available, for ease in making insertions and changes.

- Keep dated samples of your child's school papers in a separate notebook.

- Never leave your notebook with a professional or school system for more than a day or two. Have extra copies of your chronological list of documents available for them so they can indicate which reports they want you to copy and provide to them.

Resolving Problems

Even when parents and public school officials work together cooperatively toward what each sees as an appropriate education for a child with learning disabilities, they sometimes find themselves unable to agree. Some parents who are in this predicament may decide to start due process proceedings, as provided for in the Education for All Handicapped Children Act.[12] (*See* Appendices E and F for information on Due Process Hearings.)

It is best, however, to avoid formal hearings and court actions if at all possible. They can be costly in terms of time, money, and physical and emotional well being. It is wiser to use these procedures only as a last resort. Try one last time to work with the personnel in your child's school. "You may have to become more vocal and assertive in your approach to dealing with the school"[13] when you have a major concern about the identification, evaluation or the program in which your child has been placed. First, meet informally with your child's teacher or teachers and the school principal. Examples of concerns that might prompt you to ask for a conference are: (1) your child seems bored, restless or angry in the resource room and you think the youngster needs a more challenging program; (2) you have moved into a new home so that your child now needs transportation, and you'd like that written into the I.E.P., or (3) you feel your child is in an improper educational setting.

As mentioned earlier in this chapter, your state's Protection and Advocacy agency is available to help resolve disputes before the due process procedure is begun (*see* Appendix C).

In some situations you may want to file a **Complaint** with your state's Department of Education, known officially as the State Education Agency (SEA). A complaint may be appropriate where you feel that the school system is failing to follow proper procedures, such as not providing services already stipulated in an IEP, improperly maintaining records, etc. Generally, a complaint focuses upon noncompliance of procedures, not questions of a substantive or qualitative nature. Your complaint must be filed in writing, after which the SEA will investigate and resolve the complaint. This resolution, upon request, may later be reviewed by the U.S. Secretary of Education at the federal level.

If your concern is in regard to substantive matters such as whether your child is or is not LD, whether your child is or is not receiving an appropriate education, whether your child needs a more or less restrictive setting, etc., then you may either file for a due process hearing (*see below*) and/or ask for **Mediation** by contacting the individual within your school system who supervises the special education services. Mediation is usually a review of your concerns by higher administrative level officials within the school system. It is important to remember that mediation may not be used to deny or delay your right to a due process hearing.[14]

If mediation fails, your next recourse is to write your school division superintendent, with a copy to your state's Department of Education, requesting a **Due Process Hearing**. This letter should outline the dispute, summarize any action you have already taken, and request that the due process hearing be scheduled. Meanwhile, try to talk to other parents who have been through due process hearings. Also, you may want to contact local parent or advocacy groups (*see* Appendix B). Ask them for assistance. They can often provide support and information to help you prepare for due process.

Parents who have a due process hearing may, by their manner, help to make the experience more successful. For example, it is a good idea to address your testimony to the Hearing Officer. Develop rapport and eye contact with this person. Listen carefully to questions; take time when answering. In being cross-examined, do not argue. Always address your response to the Hearing Officer. Do not refer to "best programs," "optimal performance," or "reaching maximum potential." The law only speaks to an "appropriate program" sufficient to confer some educational benefit. Use real-life experiences to help paint a picture of your child. Do not volunteer unsolicited information. Pay close attention to questions from the Hearing Officer. While this could be your opportunity to elaborate on a point, be sure that your elaboration will not be detrimental to your case. Recognize that the local school division will have an attorney well versed in the field of special education and the law itself. If you are not represented by an attorney, be sure that you are familiar with the current case law that applies to your unique set of facts.

The due process hearing is a quasi judicial proceeding in which decisions are based upon the facts of the case (testimony, documents, other evidence) and the law (statutes, regulations, and constantly changing case law). If you disagree with the results of the hearing, you may request a Review of the decision. A

Reviewing Officer will be appointed to conduct a **Review Hearing**. At his discretion he may or may not hear additional or new evidence. He will, however read the trial transcript, exhibits, legal briefs, and the due process decision, and then issue his written report that will either affirm or reverse the earlier decision of the Hearing Officer.

Either party may then appeal an adverse decision by filing a civil suit in either the local state court or the U.S. District Court.

It may be advisable for you to retain private sector professionals who can evaluate your position prior to your initiating a due process hearing. The Education for All Handicapped Children Act, as amended August 5, 1986, authorizes parents who prevail to be reimbursed for legal fees and other costs, under certain circumstances (20 U.S.C. Section 1415 (e)(4)(E)).

Due process can be a protracted, difficult struggle. But sometimes in terms of what is right for your child, it is a recommended step to take.

(*See* Appendix E for more details about compliance and the Due Process Hearing system.)

[1]Lillie, D. and Place, P. (1982). *Partners - A guide to working with schools for parents of children with special instructional needs.* Glenview, IL: Scott, Foresman & Co.

[2]*Ibid.*

[3]*Ibid.*

[4]National Information Center for Handicapped Children and Youth. (1987). Procedural safeguards insuring that handicapped children receive a free appropriate public education. *NICHCY News Digest.* Washington, DC: Author.

[5]Lillie, D. and Place, P. (1982). op. cit.

[6]National Information Center for Handicapped Children and Youth. (1984). *NICHCY News Digest.* Washington, DC: Author.

[7]National Information Center for Handicapped Children and Youth. (1977). *Closer Look.* Fall, 1977. Washington, DC: Author.

[8]*Ibid.*

[9]Lillie, D. and Place, P. (1982). op. cit.

[10]National Information Center for Handicapped Children and Youth. *Closer Look,* op. cit.

[11]Craig, T. (1984). Especially for parents—Don't wait and see! *Their World.* New York: Foundation for Children with Learning Disabilities.

[12]Parent Educational Advocacy Training Center. (1987). Handicapped Children's Protection Act of 1986—The attorney's fee bill. *Parent Center News,* September, 1987. Alexandria, VA: Author.

[13]Lillie, D. and Place, P. (1982). op. cit.

[14]*Ibid.*

Make It Happen With Positive Parent Advocacy

— Getting Involved —

Have You...	Yes	No
● joined the PTA?	____	____
● attended the PTA meetings? (joining is only the first step)	____	____
● become a room volunteer? (your child loves to have you at school)	____	____
● accompanied the class on a field trip? (pack good walking shoes)	____	____
● volunteered to help with a special school project? (fund raisers, athletics, carnival)	____	____
● attended special education advisory or school board meetings?	____	____
● offered to do something special for the class or school?	____	____
● complimented school personnel? (everybody likes to hear nice things)	____	____

The more **Yes** answers, the more you are on the road to positive, involved advocacy. Remember, your attitude and commitment to the overall school program demonstrate your support.

Tracking the Special Education Process

Instructions

Federal and state regulations stipulate the steps which must be followed in order to determine whether a child is LD; they also establish time limits for each step. Use the following chart to track your child's progress through the procedure.

Your Record	**The Special Education Process**
	Referral
Date of referral _____	Referral is made to the principal or special education coordinator.
Referral made by: _____	
	_____ Days*
Date of Child Study Committee Meeting _____	**Child Study Committee Meeting**
	Child Study Committee reviews the referral to determine what should be done and if formal evaluation is needed.
Did you receive a copy of the decision?_____ • If not, call and ask for a copy.	
	_____ Days*
	Referral For Formal Evaluation
	Formal Evaluation
Date you gave permission for evaluation _____	Parent permission is secured and testing is conducted.
	_____ Days*
Date of Eligibility Meeting _____	**Eligibility Committee Meeting**
Did you receive a copy of the reports?_____ Did you receive a summary or record of the meeting? _____ • If not, call and ask for a copy.	The Eligibility Committee studies and discusses the evaluations to determine if the student is handicapped and in need of special education.
	30 Calendar Days
Date of IEP Meeting _____	**IEP Committee Meeting**
	The IEP Committee, including the parent as a team member, designs the student's program.
Did you receive a copy of the IEP? _____ • If not, call and ask for a copy.	
	As Soon As Possible
	Services Begin
Date child entered program _____	Parent permission is secured and special education begins.

*NOTE: Prior to using this page, contact your state's Department of Education or Protection and Advocacy Agency to determine the timeframes mandated by the regulations in your state. Fill in the number of days accordingly.

Understanding Educational and Psychological Evaluations

Instructions

It is important that you, as a parent, fully understand the results of educational and psychological evaluations, as they will be the basis for decisions about your child's identification as LD and the types of services provided.

Any time your child is tested, whether by the public schools or by a private agency, it is most important that you meet with those individuals who completed the evaluations, so that they may review the test results with you.

Use the form on pp. 65–67 to help you organize and take notes at this meeting. Use it to help you ask questions. If you are concerned that you will have difficulty listening, asking questions and taking notes at the same time, ask your spouse, a friend, or parent advocate to take notes, using the form, while you ask questions. You might begin the meeting by showing the form to the professionals present and telling them you are going to use it to take notes during the meeting to help you better understand their test results.

As each professional discusses his test results, ask him to:

- Name the particular test given.

- Describe exactly what the test evaluates. Some tests have many different subtests which measure various skills; ask him to describe each. **Be certain to ask questions now if any terms or educational jargon are unclear.**

- Give an example of the types of questions on the test, what your child had to do, etc. For instance, the evaluator may tell you that a particular test was given to test your child's spelling skills. You need to know whether your child had to actually write the correct spelling of words, indicate the correct spelling when given several choices, or spell the word aloud, etc.

- Describe how your child performed on this particular test or subtest when compared to other children of the same age and/or grade level. In other words, does your child seem to have a problem in the skills evaluated by this test when compared to others of the same age/grade?

- Describe how your child performed on this particular test or subtest given his own particular

ability or general intelligence level. Not all children have the same ability. It is important to know not just how your child compares to **other children** (the item discussed above), but also how he does on a particular skill compared to **his own ability**. In other words, is your child doing the best that we might expect on a particular skill, given his own ability, or is he doing more poorly than we would expect, given his ability.

(You may want to duplicate several copies of the first page of the form so that you will have sufficient space for notes if many tests were given.)

Once the evaluator has described the individual tests, use the questions on the last page of the form to help guide your discussion to pull all the information together. If the evaluator does not offer this information on his own, do not hesitate to ask the specific questions suggested.

Throughout your meetings and discussions about the test results, keep the following in mind:

- **Ask questions when you do not understand what is being said.** Without a thorough understanding of the test results, you will be unable to actively participate in planning and monitoring your child's educational program.

- **Do not pay attention to test scores reported as grade equivalents or age equivalents** [e.g., if someone says your child tested on a 5.3 grade level (5th grade, 3rd month of school) or at a 7.4 year old level (7 years, 4 months old)]. Due to the manner in which these scores are calculated, they are very easily misinterpreted. In fact, many professionals and professional organizations no longer use grade or age equivalents at all.

As soon as possible after the meeting, review your notes. If you have any questions about terminology, refer to the glossary of this handbook. If you still have questions, contact the evaluator to clarify them. Once you are certain that you understand your notes, file them with a copy of the actual evaluation. Use this information to help plan for the IEP and/or if you plan to contest the school's recommendations.

Note: If your child has already been tested and you have already met with the evaluator(s) to review the test results, complete the forms on pp. 65–67 by yourself, referring to a copy of the evaluations. If you are unable to do this, you do not have a good understanding of the test results. **Request another meeting; use the forms and ask questions**.

Summary of _____ Evaluation Review for _____

(Psychological or Educational)   (Your Child's Name)

Date Tests Administered _____ Name of Evaluator _____

Date of Review Meeting _____ Individuals Present _____

Test Results:

Name of Test	What Does It Test?	Example	How Did My Child Do Compared to Others Same Age/Grade Level?	How Did My Child Do Compared to Own Ability/ General Intelligence Level?

Summary of _____
(Psychological or Educational)

Date Tests Administered _____

Date of Review Meeting _____

Conclusions:

1. What are my child's weaknesses compared to others of the same age/grade level?

2. What are my child's own individual weaknesses compared to his own ability/general intelligence level? Are these weaknesses different from those noted in question #1?

3. What are my child's strengths compared to others of the same age/grade level?

4. What are my child's own individual strengths compared to his own ability/general intelligence level?

5. What are the recommendations based on these test results?

Evaluation Review for _____
(Your Child's Name)

Name of Evaluator _____

Individuals Present _____

6. Is there a need for further testing? Are there any remaining questions about my child?

7. Do the test results indicate that my child is learning disabled? Why or why not?

8. According to the test results, how will my child probably progress in the present classroom placement? Can we anticipate that he/she will do well or poorly?

9. Do the test results indicate a need for special help? If so, in what?

Pre-IEP Planning Form for Parents

DIRECTIONS:

Below are some of the questions and concerns often voiced by parents before and during the IEP meeting. We share them with you in order to encourage you to identify your own concerns or areas where clarification would be helpful. Check any items that you too have thought about and write in others that you wish to discuss at the upcoming IEP meeting

	Responses	Comments and Other Questions
I. Questions relating to information collected for the eligibility decisions		
___ 1. What do the terms		
(specify terms you want clarified)		
that were used in the assessment report mean?		
___ 2. Without this learning disability, where would you expect my child to be functioning, based on all the tests that were given?		
___ 3. If my child is really reading below level, how can I ever expect him/her to pass his/her other school subjects?		
___ 4. What does all this information mean in terms of the future? Can we expect our child to pass minimum competency tests? What special help will be provided for my child if he/she can't read this exam? Should we plan on college? What special help will be provided for my child if he/she wants to take the college entrance exams?		
Other questions (jot down what's on your mind)		
5.		

—69—

Reproduced with permission from *Learning Disabilities: Understanding Concepts, Characteristics and Issues* by Houck, C. & Geller, C. (Englewood Cliffs: Prentice-Hall, Inc., 1984)

	Responses	Comments and Other Questions
6.		
7.		
8.		

II. Questions relating to specialized services

___ 1. How *much* special service will be needed given the severity of my child's disability?

___ 2. Looking at my child's progress, the gains have been meager (i.e., 3 or 4 months per year). Is this the best we can hope for? Would more help per day result in greater gains?

___ 3. Who will provide the service(s)?

___ 4. What specifically needs to be provided? What do you believe is of highest priority at this time (e.g., reading, written work, math, spelling, etc.)?

___ 5. Where will the specialized instruction take place? At this school?

___ 6. How many other students will be with my child and what are their needs?

___ 7. What regular classes will be missed while he/she is with the LD teacher?

	Responses	Comments and Other Questions

____ 8. What will be my child's daily schedule?

____ 9. How much time will the LD teacher spend each day with my child? Are there any other services that he/she may need (e.g., speech therapy, adapted physical education, counseling, etc.)?

____ 10. Will the methods and materials used in the LD classroom be different from those the regular teachers use? If so, please explain the differences.

____ 11. What is it about how my child learns that makes these different methods or materials better?

____ 12. How will my child's regular classroom activities relate to the LD program?

____ 13. With so many teachers, who is going to coordinate what is happening in my child's school day?

____ 14. How soon will I know if the program is working? If I am concerned about whether or not the program is working, can I suggest changes in the program or can I remove my child from the program?

____ 15. If this were your child, would you consider the program we have discussed one that would meet his/her needs?

____ 16. What can I do at home to help?

	Responses	Comments and Other Questions
17. What happens next?		
Other concerns (Jot down points you want to discuss) 18.		
19.		
20.		
21.		

III. Expectations (parent "wish list")

____ 1. In thinking about your child and his/her comprehensive educational needs, list any specific things you want the school to provide that you feel might be overlooked (e.g., specific interests).

____ 2. Indicate any comments your child has expressed which you believe should be considered as we plan the IEP.

3. *Other*

Individualized Education Program (IEP)

Blueprint to Your Child's Program

The IEP is the most important meeting and document written for your child. Use this parent worksheet to prepare for it.

(Circle one)

Before any meeting ...

- Have you told your child about the meeting?   YES   NO
  ("Hey it's my life, too.")

- Have you organized your thoughts?   YES   NO
  (*See* Pre-IEP Planning Form)

Before an initial IEP or an eligibility/IEP meeting ...

- Have you asked for evaluation reports at least   YES   NO
  one week prior to the meeting?

- Did the school system provide you the reports?   YES   NO

If NO, ask to stop the process until you have the reports. It is important that you have the information ahead of time. Having the reports at least one week in advance will give you the opportunity to review the information and reports before the meeting. It's a good idea to tell the school personnel early that you want the reports before the meeting to give them time to have the reports ready.

- Have you read and highlighted important points   YES   NO
  or any area you have concerns about or don't
  understand?

At the meeting ...

- Do you know the names and titles of those present?   YES   NO
  (If no, stop and ask for introductions.)

- Do you have a copy of the plan to follow or could   YES   NO
  you read along with the teacher?

- If annual review, do you have a copy with you   YES   NO
  of last year's IEP to update? (Were goals and
  objectives met? Should some be continued, etc.?)

- Have you shared your observations, goals,   YES   NO
  and expectations from your Pre-IEP Planning Form?

- Have you complimented the school system   YES   NO
  personnel on the plan, their work, etc.?
  (Everyone likes to hear good things.)

After the meeting ...

- Did you present your concerns in a positive way?　　　　YES　　　　　NO

- Did you ask for help in areas where you have a concern?　　YES　　　　　NO

- Did you ask how you can help at home?　　　　　　　　YES　　　　　NO

- Have you reviewed the plan with your child?　　　　　YES　　　　　NO

- Have you received reports on progress?　　　　　　　YES　　　　　NO

- Have you contacted the teacher and/or principal
  with questions or concerns?　　　　　　　　　　　　YES　　　　　NO

- Did you support the IEP?　　　　　　　　　　　　　YES　　　　　NO

- Have you followed through with the home-family
  commitment?　　　　　　　　　　　　　　　　　　YES　　　　　NO

- Have you completed the "Post IEP Meeting Checklist"
  which follows before signing the IEP?　　　　　　　YES　　　　　NO

Remember, set a tone of positive support and advocacy.

Post-IEP Meeting Checklist

DIRECTIONS:
Before signing your youngster's IEP, use this checklist, item by item, to review the contents of the IEP. Those items indicated with an * are required by law to be included in the IEP. Your response to each item should be "yes." If you are unable to answer "yes," make note of any questions in the comment section and clarify with school professionals before signing the IEP.

	YES or NO	COMMENTS or QUESTIONS
I. PRESENT LEVELS OF EDUCATIONAL PERFORMANCE		
*1. Is there up-to-date information on the level of your child's skills in basic academic (oral language, listening, reading word attack, reading comprehension, spelling, written expression, math calculation, problem solving), study, emotional, social, behavioral and/or vocational skills to document every area of weakness?		
2. If standardized tests are used to document skill levels, are test names, dates administered and standardized test scores included?		
3. If teacher observation is used to document skill levels, are specific descriptions of what the student can (or can't) do, under what circumstances, included, as well as the date(s) observed?		
II. ANNUAL GOALS AND SHORT TERM OBJECTIVES		
*1. Are there annual goals included for every identified area of weakness documented in I (1) above?		
*2. For each annual goal, are there a series of shorter term, specific objectives that, taken together, outline the sequence of steps needed to achieve the annual goal?		

	YES or NO	COMMENTS or QUESTIONS
3. Do the short term objectives specifically state what the child will do/learn and how we will know whether or not he has learned it? (Key Words: % accuracy, _(number)_ out of _(number)_ correct, _(number)_ out of _(number)_ attempts, etc.) Example of poorly written objective: "Johnny will learn the alphabet." Example of specific, behavioral objective: "When shown flash cards with individual letters of the alphabet, Johnny will (a) say the name of the letter and (b) provide the sound of the letter with 100% accuracy on 3 out of 4 attempts."		
4. Is an example word, comprehension question, math problem which illustrates the objective included?		
5. Is there space provided to include the date when instruction for a specific objective is started and when mastery is demonstrated?		
6. Is there provision for the reporting of progress relative to the objectives during the year?		
III. SPECIFIC EDUCATIONAL SERVICES		
1. Is my child's handicapping condition designated as a "specific learning disability?"		
2. Is the type of special education program or organizational model indicated, i.e., "LD Resource Program," "LD Self-Contained Program," etc.?		
*3. Are the number of hours per day and the subject/content areas covered in the special education program designated?		
*4. Are the number of hours per day and the subject/content areas in the regular education program designated?		
5. Is the location at which services will be provided designated?		

	YES or NO	COMMENTS or QUESTIONS
*6. Is the provision of transportation to the service location designated, if needed?		
7. Are any special accommodations, needed in regular or special classes, designated, i.e., oral tests, longer time to complete assignments, availability of a word processor, etc.?		
8. Is the date included for my child's participation in any state required testing programs, as well as any special accommodations needed? If no date is noted, is there a statement re: exemption from testing?		
9. For high school students, is there a statement included as to whether the student is working towards graduation in a diploma granting program or a certificate of attendance?		
*10. Are any related services needed for my child to benefit from special education designated, i.e., counseling, physical, occupational or speech therapy, etc.?		
11. Is there any one individual at the school designated to coordinate my child's services and the various professionals working with him?		
*12. Are projected dates for the start of services and anticipated duration of services included?		
IV. ANNUAL REVIEW		
*1. Is a date included (at least once a school year) indicating when the IEP Committee will meet again to examine the child's progress relative to the IEP?		
*2. Is there a statement indicating how progress will be evaluated?		
3. Will the same methods/tests administered to assess levels of educational performance (I of this Checklist) be re-administered for the sake of comparison?		

	YES or NO	COMMENTS or QUESTIONS
V. TRANSITION SERVICES *1. For students 14 years of age or older, are plans, with specific goals and objectives, included to help the student move from the school environment to the "real world"? (Depending on the individual student, these may include activities and objectives designed to help the student access successfully vocational training, higher education, independent living training, etc.).		
*2. For students 14 years of age or older, is there a description of what other agencies, besides the school, will assist with transition services and what exactly they will do?		
VI. MISCELLANEOUS 1. Are the names and signatures of all individuals participating in the development of the IEP included?		
2. Do you have a copy of the IEP?		

LD Teenagers

Instructions

If your child is a preteen or teen, you need to involve him or her in the development of the IEP. This is important for two reasons. First, your child's own insights and observations about school **are** very important and should be incorporated into the IEP. In addition, LD students need to learn to begin to take responsibility for managing their own problems. They need to recognize that coming to grips with their learning disabilities is indeed their responsibility, as well as that of their parents and teachers.

Work the following puzzle **with** your LD teenager.

Then use the checklist which follows the puzzle to determine how you're doing as a parent of a teenager.

I'm a Puzzle

Help your parents get to know you better. Work this puzzle together to give them information.

I'm good at … _____ _____ _____	This school work is easy for me … _____ _____ My favorite subject is _____
I need help with … _____ _____ _____	This school work is hard for me … _____ _____ _____
My favorite time is … _____ _____	My best study time is … _____ _____
My favorite things are … _____ _____ I like to _____ _____ _____	I need quiet to study Yes _____ No _____ I like to write what I study. It helps me remember. Yes _____ No _____

Hey! It's My Life, Too!

Before the IEP meeting, have you ...

- Explained to your teenager the importance of
  the IEP meeting and what the meeting is about?   YES   NO

- Asked your youngster to tell you what's good
  at school and what's not so hot?   YES   NO

- Reassured your youngster that everybody is
  working together to help make learning easier?   YES   NO
  ("It's team work between the school and family.")

- Outlined your teenager's strengths?   YES   NO
  (Everyone needs to hear the good stuff! Pointing out
  strong points builds confidence.)

- Asked your youngster to participate in the meeting?   YES   NO

After the IEP meeting, have you ...

- Set up a planned time for going over the program?   YES   NO
  (Review the program even if your child attended
  the meeting, to clarify points and reexplain the plan.)

- Organized your home program for involvement   YES   NO
  including responsibilities for homework, classwork, etc.?

- Shown your support for the program and IEP?   YES   NO
  ("At the meeting today everyone really worked together
  on this special program.")

Remember, your teenager needs to be a part of the decision-making. Involvement in the IEP is one
step toward development of ownership of learning. It helps lay the groundwork for accepting
responsibility. Make sure you answered <u>YES</u> to the questions above.

Report Organizer For Child's Reports

Instructions

Organize material in chronological order. File the most recent reports first. To help keep track of the reports and keep your file in order, put the author's name and date of the report in the lower right hand corner. Then fill out and file this form in front of the reports.

Date of Report	Evaluator or Author	Description	Summary

Telephone–Visit Log

Instructions

Keeping track of your communications is easier if you make notes immediately following the conversation or visit. Take a few minutes each time to record your calls and visits. Do this for **every** phone call or meeting.

Date/Time	Conversation/ Visit With ...	Reason	Important Points

V. Planning For The Future

Transition and Vocational Guidance

Many learning disabled young people who have graduated from high school may still have trouble finding work or entering post-secondary environments. They may continue to experience difficulties academically, socially or emotionally. Often there are federal, state and community resources available to ease the transition from high school. Many of these resources are included in Appendices B and G of this book.

Looking Ahead

Of utmost importance in facilitating the transition for a learning disabled young person from high school to the "real world" is planning. Certainly before the completion of the student's first year in high school, the student, his parents, guidance counselor, LD teacher and other school personnel should meet to discuss post-secondary considerations and options.

Early in the student's high school experience, decisions must be made to determine whether the immediate goal following high school is employment, college or an alternative post-secondary program specifically for the learning disabled (*see* Appendices B and G). The decision-making process should be a team effort involving the student, parents and school personnel. Considerations should not be limited to just an assessment of the student's strengths and weaknesses (although this is certainly important), but should also recognize the student's interests, motivation and desire to attain his goals. These decisions should be integrated into the student's IEP. Goals and objectives on the IEP during the remaining high school years should represent a well thought out, comprehensive plan that will, at the completion of high school, enable the student to move on successfully to a job, college or other post-secondary placement.

Fostering Independence

At this point, it is important to emphasize that, regardless of a student's specific post-secondary goals, it is critical that the high school program build the LD student's independence. Parents and teachers alike must work towards decreasing the LD student's dependence on others, while teaching him the skills to advocate for himself. This is not something that will happen overnight nor will it happen "automatically"—it must be taught. With parents' and teachers' help, the

LD student must learn to evaluate his own strengths and weaknesses and be able to describe his learning disability to others. He must learn to identify the strategies which help him to work around his disability, as well as to identify any accommodations he may need to succeed in his different classes. He should gradually assume responsibility for seeking those accommodations from classroom teachers, rather than depending solely upon the initiation of the LD teacher or his parents. Certainly, he should also be an active participant in all IEP and other meetings relative to planning his future.

The need to overtly teach the LD student skills which allow him to exercise his independence cannot be overemphasized. To do otherwise, either consciously or not, perpetuates the cycle of "learned helplessness," which, in turn, leads to a young adult totally dependent on others to assist him.

Vocational Guidance

While college may be an option for some LD individuals (see the section which immediately follows in this chapter), others choose to pursue vocational training, hoping to secure a job following high school. Planning is again important and a good plan depends upon a thorough evaluation of the student's aptitudes and abilities.

A vocational assessment may be conducted by the school and/or the Department of Rehabilitative Services (*see* Appendix C for a state-by-state listing). Once the evaluation has been completed, vocational and guidance counselors should meet with the student, his parents and the LD teacher to explore the test results in light of the student's career interests.

The student's IEP should be written to include goals

and objectives in job training in the student's chosen career. These goals may then be accomplished through participation in the school's Vocational-Technical Center, special "on-the-job" placement and training supervised by school personnel and any other programs available in your school system. Parents should know that a federal law called the Carl D. Perkins Vocational Education Act (P.L. 98–154), as well as Section 504 of the Rehabilitation Act of 1973, guarantees that learning disabled students shall have access to all regular vocational education programs available in the public schools. For example, a student's reading disability, and subsequent difficulty in reading the training manual in an auto mechanics class, does not mean that he cannot/should not take this class. Rather, accommodations must be made to allow the student to acquire the information in the manual by some means other than reading.

It should also be noted that the IEP should emphasize job-seeking and interpersonal skills, as well as specific job training. LD students must learn how to locate available positions, complete job applications, participate in an interview, etc. Likewise, the importance of interpersonal skills—being on time, knowing how to speak and relate to a supervisor or co-workers, etc.—are also increasingly recognized as critical to the success of the young person's adjustment.

Resources

As noted earlier, federal, state and community resources are available to learning disabled individuals seeking training and employment. One starting point might be the *HEATH Resource Center* (Higher Education and Adult Training for People with Handicaps). The center provides a wealth of information, at no charge, about training and post-secondary opportunities for learning disabled young people. Their toll-free telephone number is listed in Appendix B.

The *Department of Rehabilitative Services*, with offices in every state (*see* Appendix C), has programs which may be of benefit to the learning disabled. Clients must be 15 years old, but there is no maximum age limit. Training is provided in over 50 job areas, as well as in work adjustment, job seeking and independent living. Vocational evaluation is comprehensive and can include counseling and guidance, standardized testing, psychological testing, work sample evaluations, vocational exploration and job analysis. Fees for these services operate on a sliding scale, based on one's ability to pay.

Assistance may also be available through the *Job Training Assistance Program* (JTAP), administered by the U.S. Department of Labor (*see* Appendix B for a

central phone number to identify services in your area). Both academic and vocational opportunities may be available through this program, ranging from college-level courses to remediation in basic skills. Programs may be offered through community colleges, business colleges and trade schools.

Your state *Employment Commission* can also provide testing to determine aptitude and ability for those seeking work.

Opportunities through the local public schools may be available even for those beyond school age or those who have left school. Many LD students continue to need basic skills instruction. Those who elect to enter *Adult Basic Education* (ABE) Programs may prove to be more receptive or ready than they were the first time they were in school, being more mature, finding a more practical emphasis placed on academics and working with more mature classmates. In addition to ABE programs, special services or programs for the learning disabled young adult may be available through the local Vocational–Technical Center in your school system. Contact the Adult Education and Vocational Education departments in area school systems.

Jobs, Paid and Volunteer

Registering with a *temporary employment* service may be easier for the youth who fears rejection in the job market than applying for and being interviewed for a specific job with a particular company. The temporary employee often does not need the level of skill a full-time employee must exhibit. This may lessen the pressure while the young person learns about the world of work from the "inside."

A *volunteer position* is sometimes the answer for one not sure of his or her ability to retain a paid job. Here, almost any effort is appreciated and some skills can be learned while confidence is being built. Sometimes volunteer positions can evolve into paid employment.

If none of these avenues seem likely to work and you consider your young person unemployable, it might be wise to check with the Social Security Administration and the Department of Public Welfare's SSI division. They will advise you if any funds are available for the support of your child. A caution: It is difficult for parents to be objective about their own children; this applies to their conclusions concerning their child's employability. Therefore, it is well to listen carefully to the opinions of those individuals and services consulted. Another factor to be considered is that the process of determining need for financial assistance for a handicapped person is quite rigorous.

College for the LD Student

According to a recent survey, 62.2 percent of high school graduates will continue with their education.[1] Before graduation, these students talk to counselors, read brochures, visit campuses, and take admission tests. Hopes are high for acceptance to "their" college. But what about the learning disabled student? While college is not appropriate for many LD students, for others it is a realistic goal. According to Margaret Dietz Meyer, those learning disabled students who succeed in college seem to possess the following characteristics:

- "Ability to articulate one's special talents and abilities clearly

- Knowledge of the nature of one's learning disability, and of the kinds of teaching strategies, tools, and services which best help one compensate

- Ability to explain both special talents and needed compensatory strategies, clearly and frankly, to adults

- Maturity and initiative to assume the greater share of one's own advocacy

- Adherence to effective, routine study habits, to whatever degree is necessary for success

- Acceptance of the need to seek assistance for academic and other problems, as appropriate

- Initiative to seek such assistance

- Acceptance of the idea that it may take one longer to graduate than one's friends, and that one may have to study harder than they seem to do

- Recognition of the concept that college is meant to be a challenge, and that temporary frustrations are part of the normal growth process

- Regular, frequent communication with parents, friends, classroom professors, academic advisor, and support service teacher."[2]

It has also been observed that college level LD students must be self-reliant, able to cope with the ever-changing challenges of daily living. LD students who have learned to rely heavily on both parents and teachers to direct them and manage their lives may have difficulty adjusting to the demands of college life.[3]

The task for the student is to find a college that will stress and develop special interests, talents, and abilities, and at the same time be respectful and supportive of special needs. This often has to go beyond superficial support and a sympathetic attitude; continued remediation as well as accommodations are important for many LD students in order for them to be able to complete their college careers.

Colleges are prohibited by Section 504 of the Rehabilitation Act of 1973 from discriminating against learning disabled students in recruitment, testing, admissions, and treatment after admission. Post-secondary institutions are required to make reasonable adjustments to permit handicapped students to fulfill academic requirements.[4] Today, many colleges accept LD students and make such adjustments. (*See* Appendix G.) Some strategies that seem to help learning disabled college students are untimed testing, access to tutors, provision of note-takers and readers, use of tape recorders, and access to word processors. The key in this situation is to find just the right school for your individual child's needs, interests, and personality.

In comparing and evaluating colleges, parents and students may want to consider the following questions:[5,6]

Admissions Requirements

- Should the LD student file for admission with or without declaring a learning disability as a handicap? If the student declares the handicap at the time of admissions, additional information may be accepted which would enhance consideration for entry. This decision should be made in conjunction with advisors familiar with the student's strengths and weaknesses.

- What entrance examinations are required and are modifications in test administration acceptable? For example, is it possible for LD students to take the SATs untimed and/or with a reader? Arrangements would be made with the student's guidance counselor and/or LD teacher.

- What, if any, minimum academic standing must the LD student have achieved in high school? The LD student should be competitive with at least the average student enrolled at the college, given minimal accommodations.

- Are there specific course requirements for admission (e.g., foreign language requirement), and can these requirements be waived?

Matriculation Requirements

- Are special classes provided in basic skills, study habits, time management, note taking?

- Are individual tutoring and counseling provided and does one pay extra for these services?

- Are special study services available, such as taped books, word processors, note takers, etc.?

- Is the director of the support program trained in learning disabilities?[7]

- Can professors and classes be hand-scheduled?

- What are the requirements for program completion?

- May a student take a lighter than usual course load?

Perhaps most important when considering a particular school, prospective students and parents should talk with other LD students who are attending or have attended the school, and with their parents. Their personal experiences may prove enlightening.

Appendix G includes a list of directories and other sources of information about college and post-secondary programs for learning disabled students. Again, it must be emphasized that the key is finding a program which best meets your child's needs.

Ask questions. Talk to other parents and students. Remember that the programs and services provided by individual colleges vary greatly. Do not necessarily restrict your search to those colleges which indicate they have specific services for learning disabled students. Some small colleges which are attuned to the needs of individual students may be appropriate, depending upon the student.

Once a student has selected and been accepted to a college, the following information should be kept in mind:[8,9]

- Assist your youngster in selecting appropriate campus housing, if planning to live away from home. A small residence hall, preferably with an older student or other individual as an advisor, may be more conducive to studying and maintaining a stable environment than a large dormitory or an apartment.

- Prepare a duplicate copy of the most current testing data and any other pertinent files you have kept, for your son or daughter to take to college. Your LD young person will need to act as his or her own advocate now, and may need this information to document the necessity of certain accommodations, etc.

- Assist in compiling necessary aids, in addition to the usual college paraphernalia. This should include a calendar and address book, as well as dictionary, calculator, tape recorder, and computer accessories (depending on what may also be available at the college).

- Encourage your youngster to: attend the summer orientation program and ask questions; meet with the assigned advisor to plan the upcoming class schedule; ask how instructors of different sections teach a particular course. Also, suggest speaking to individual instructors, reviewing course outlines, and checking in the bookstore to find out how much reading is required for specific courses.

- Let your child know that college is a big adjustment for all students. Encourage asking the designated support service personnel for help if needed. Let your young person know you are always available for moral support!

[1] After high school: College. (1985). *Lead.* October, 1985, p. 1.

[2] Dietz Meyer, M. (1988). Get ready for college. *Their World.* New York: Foundation for Children with Learning Disabilities, pp. 62–63.

[3] Vogel, S. (1987). LD students in college need self-knowledge. *Update,* Vol. 1, No. 2. Chevy Chase, MD: Tri-Services, Inc.

[4] Scheiber. B. and Talpen, J. (1985). *Campus access for learning disabled students.* Washington, DC. National Information Center for Handicapped Children and Youth, pp. 3–4.

[5] Westhead. E. (1980). *Postsecondary education for the LD student—A few suggestions.* A paper prepared for the Virginia Association for Children and Adults with Learning Disabilities, Richmond, VA.

[6] Dietz Meyer, M. (1988). op. cit.

[7] Foundation for Children with Learning Disabilities. (1985). *The FCLD Learning Disabilities Resource Guide.* New York: Author.

[8] Westhead, E. op. cit.

[9] Dietz Meyer, M. (1988). op. cit.

A Checklist for Parents and Students Considering College

College catalogues are written for general audiences and may not indicate clearly all special support systems that are available or communicate fully flexible attitudes and policies which may be of help to the learning disabled student. If a visit to the college and an appointment with an admissions counselor is not possible, a phone call or letter which asks specific questions may still be of great help. Following are some suggested questions:

Name of Person Contacted _____ **College** _____

Entrance Requirements

What, if any, entrance examinations must the student take? _____

_____

_____

Can any of these exams be waived? _____

_____

_____

Is the untimed Scholastic Aptitude Test acceptable?

_____

_____

_____

Is a minimum score required on any of these tests?

_____

_____

_____

_____

What, if any, minimum academic standing must the student have achieved in high school?

_____

_____

_____

Are there specific course requirements (such as foreign language study) for admission?

_____

_____

_____

_____

If so, can any of these requirements be waived? Or can other courses be substituted (e.g., substitute sign language for the deaf or a computer language for a foreign language)?

_____

_____

_____

_____

Is admission limited to certain fields of study only?

_____

_____

_____

Matriculation Requirements

Once the student has been accepted, what provisions can be made for him and what support services are available? _____

_____

_____

_____

What are the specific requirements for program completion?

_____

_____

_____

Can any of these requirements be waived?

_____

_____

Can a student take a lighter-than-usual course load?

_____

_____

_____

Must the student complete the program in a specified length of time? _____

_____

_____

Can the student tape-record classes?

_____

_____

Are oral examinations possible?

_____

_____

_____

What kinds of tutorial services are available?

_____

_____

_____

_____

Would such service involve any extra expense?

_____

_____

_____

What is the average class size? _____

_____

_____

_____

What kinds of special counseling are available?

_____

_____

_____

Is there a learning center, resource room, or learning lab on campus? _____

_____

_____

_____

Has the college accepted learning disabled students in the past? _____

_____

_____

Have these students been successful?_____

_____

_____

The Young Adult – Social Aspects

It has been stressed in previous sections of this handbook that a learning disability can make a life-long impact on an individual, in non-academic as well as academic aspects of living, since it can affect areas of self-esteem, interpersonal relationships, and daily living skills needed for independence.[1]

Positive personality traits—perseverance, ambition, optimism, willingness to try hard, eagerness to continue even after failure, and willingness to ask for and receive help—such traits help us through life, whether or not we're learning disabled.

But an LD young adult can have these traits and still be unsuccessful because of lack of social awareness. These young people may be less able to interpret the emotions and attitudes of others. One study found that 25 percent of the group included in the study felt they had social difficulties; however, the number could be higher since those with non-verbal disorders are not always aware of the reactions of people around them. Their problems range from general difficulty in making and keeping friends to specific problems associated with social functions. Many reported problems related with language and communication. Some said they could not follow conversations, so they tried to "fake it." Others had problems with rapid interchanges and comprehension of vocabulary. Occasionally this population would ask friends to explain things, but generally their problems made them feel insecure socially.[2]

Learning disabled young adults use a great deal of energy in managing their personal affairs. Superficially they don't appear different from the general public, but their disabilities are always with them and their uneven abilities are frustrating to themselves as well as to those around them. They often have many strengths, but their specific disorders may prevent them from realizing their potential. Their hopes and desires may not be fulfilled unless they find ways of coping.[3] Years of experience with different kinds of failure can result in a sharply diminished sense of self-worth, and this reduced self-esteem can affect a person's social interaction.

There are no fool-proof techniques for assuring that an LD child will grow into a self-assured adult. There appear to be no common characteristics of personality development for those with a learning disability.[4] Children's and young people's emotional reactions to failure will depend largely upon their beliefs about success and failure. Everyone has a unique way of handling feelings, deficiencies, and environment. However, the suggestions in Chapter III for improving a youngster's self-esteem are recommended for earnest study.

Some learning disabled young adults will weather the transitions and storms they face by themselves. Others will need the help and guidance of a parent, teacher, or a friend, or will find support in peer groups or through a buddy system. Still others may need more formalized help from a counselor or other professional.

In spite of the many difficulties with which they must cope, many learning disabled young adults become highly successful adults. (Examples are Albert Einstein, General George Patton, Nelson Rockefeller, and Thomas Edison, among others.) It has been observed that in many cases this population achieves success in life at a later age than their high-achieving peers. The stubborn persistence mentioned earlier that some LD individuals demonstrate seems to provide the resilience and the tenacity needed for success— sometimes a success even greater than that found by the non-LD population of similar ability.

[1]Scheiber, B. and Talpin, J. (1985). *Campus access for learning disabled students.* Washington, DC: National Information Center for Handicapped Children and Youth.

[2]Blalock, J. W. and Johnson, D. J. (1987). *Adults with learning disabilities.* New York: Harcourt Brace and Jovanovich.

[3]*Ibid.*

[4]Lerner, J. W. (1976). *Children with learning disabilities.* Boston: Houghton Mifflin Co.

Appendices

Appendix A

Definitions of Specific Learning Disability

The federal government has defined learning disabilities in Public Law 94–142, as amended by Public Law 101–476 (Individuals with Disabilities Education Act–IDEA) as follows:

> "Specific learning disability" means a disorder in one or more of the basic psychological processes involved in understanding or in using language, spoken or written, which may manifest itself in an imperfect ability to listen, think, speak, read, write, spell, or to do mathematical calculations. The term includes such conditions as perceptual handicaps, brain injury, minimal brain dysfunction, dyslexia, and developmental aphasia. The term does not include children who have problems which are primarily the result of visual, hearing, or motor handicaps, of mental retardation, emotional disturbance, or of environmental, cultural, or economic disadvantage.

While the above definition is included in the federal law governing the identification of LD children and the provision of services in public schools, there are variations in interpretation from state to state, and even school system to school system.

Some states and schools have tried to clarify the federal definition by adding their own specific criteria to aid in the identification of LD students. For example, some states specify an intelligence range into which students must fall in order to be considered learning disabled. Furthermore, while many state definitions include the concept of a learning disability as a discrepancy between achievement and potential, some go a step further in quantifying how large that discrepancy must be, as manifested by various test scores. It is interesting to note the lack of consensus, with each state using a slightly different "yardstick." It is not unheard of for parents who have moved from one state to another, or even one school system to another, to be told that while their child may have been labeled "learning disabled" in one locality, he may be deemed not eligible for services according to another system's criteria! In such situations parents may find it helpful to contact their state's Protection and Advocacy agency (see Appendix C).

It is important for parents to be very clear about the criteria which will be used to determine if their child is LD and therefore eligible for special education services. Contact both your state's Department of Education (see Appendix C) and your local school to request a copy of the definition and criteria which will be used in evaluating your child.

Appendix B

Information and Support Groups

NOTE: Listings are included for information purposes only. No endorsement by the Learning Disabilities Council is intended or implied.

● Adult Basic Education Program

Contact the Department of Education in your state. (*See* Appendix C)

● Adult Resources

–HEATH Resource Network   800-544-3284

–Job Accommodation Network   800-526-7234

–Learning Disabilities Association   (412) 341-1515
     of America (LDAA)
     4156 Library Road
     Pittsburgh, PA 15234

–National Center for Learning   (212) 687-7211
     Disabilities (NCLD)
     99 Park Avenue
     New York, NY 10016

–National Network of Learning   (602) 941-5112
     Disabled Adults

–Orton Dyslexia Society   800-222-3123
     724 York Road
     Baltimore, MD 21204

–President's Committee on   (202) 653-5044
     Employment of People with Disabilities
     111 20th Street, NW, Suite 636
     Washington, D.C. 20036

–U.S. Department of Labor   (202) 535-0577
     Job Training Partnership Act

● Attention Deficit Disorders Organizations

–Attention Deficit Disorders   (303) 690-7548
     Advocacy Group (ADDA)
     8091 South Ireland Way
     Aurora, CO 80016

–Children with Attention Deficit   (305) 587-3700
     Disorders (CH.A.D.D.)
     499 NW 70th Avenue, Suite 308
     Plantation, FL 33317

● Books on Tapes

–National Library Service   800-424-8567
     (state-by-state information on library books on tape for the learning disabled through state libraries for the visually and physically handicapped)

–Recording for the Blind   (609) 452-0606
     The Anne T. MacDonald Center
     20 Roszel Road
     Princeton, NJ 08540
     (textbooks on tape)

● Departments of Education—State-by-State Listing

(*See* Appendix C)

● Learning Disabilities Organizations

–Learning Disabilities Association   (412) 341-1515
     of America (LDAA)
     4156 Library Road
     Pittsburgh, PA 15234

–Learning Disabilities Council   (804) 748-5012
     Post Office Box 8451
     Richmond, VA 23226

–National Center for Learning   (212) 687-7211
     Disabilities (NCLD)
     99 Park Avenue
     New York, NY 10016

–Orton Dyslexia Society   800-222-3123
     724 York Road
     Baltimore, MD 21204

● Learning Disabilities Publications/Printed Information

–Children's Defense Fund   (202) 628-8787
     122 C Street, NW
     Washington, D.C. 20001
     (legal rights information)

–Exchange
     Learning Disabilities Network   (617) 982-8100
     25 Accord Park Drive
     Rockland, MA 02370

– Journal of Learning Disabilities   (512) 451-3246
Pro-Ed
8700 Shoal Creek Boulevard
Austin, TX 78758
(targeted for professionals)

– LDAA Booklist and LDAA   (412) 341-1515
Newsbriefs
Learning Disabilities Association of America
4156 Library Road
Pittsburgh, PA 15234

– Learning Disabilities Quarterly   (913) 492-8755
Council for Learning Disabilities
P.O. Box 40303
Overland Park, KS 66204
(targeted for professionals)

–Orton Perspectives   800-222-3123
Newsletter and Annals of Dyslexia
Orton Dyslexia Society
724 York Road
Baltimore, MD 21204

–National Information Center for   (703) 893-6061
Children and Youth with   800-999-5599
Handicaps   (recorded message)
P.O. Box 1492
Washington, D.C. 20013

–Their World (annual magazine),   (212) 687-7211
NCLD newsletter, and other information
National Center for Learning Disabilities
99 Park Avenue
New York, NY 10016

● Legal Advocacy Agencies—State-by-State Listing

(*See* Appendix C)

● Parent Training and Information Centers—State-by-State Listing

(*See* Appendix C)

● Related Parent Resources

–Parents Anonymous   800-421-0353
6733 South Sepulveda Blvd., Suite 270
Los Angeles, CA 90045
(for parents who fear they may abuse their children)

–American Speech-Language-   800-638-8255
Hearing Assoc. (ASLHA)
10801 Rockville Pike
Rockville, MD 20850

–National Institute of Neurological   (301) 496-5751
and Communication Disorders
National Institutes of Health
Building 31A, Room 8A-06
Bethesda, MD 20892

● Vocational Rehabilitation Agencies—State-by-State Listing

(*See* Appendix C)

Appendix C

State-by-State Resource Listing

While addresses and phone numbers are often subject to change, the following listings offer a "starting point" for parents in each state. Resources are listed in the following order for each state:

1. Director of Special Education/State Education Agency—can provide information and assistance regarding parents' and their handicapped child's rights under P.L. 94–142, as well as public school compliance with federal and state regulations.

2. Protection and Advocacy Agency—can provide information and assistance on all legal rights issues (identification, availability of services, accommodations, etc.) regarding the handicapped, including, but not limited to, education issues.

3. Vocational Rehabilitation Agency—can provide information and assistance in vocational assessment and training, as well as job placement and support.

4. Parent Training and Information Project(s)—can provide information on learning disabilities, local resources, as well as advocacy training for parents. Not every state has a Parent Training and Information Project; some states have several.

Alabama

Director of Special Education
Student Instructional Services
State Department of Education
500 N. Ripley
Montgomery, AL 36130
205/261-5099
205/242-8114; 800-392-8020

Program Director
Alabama Disabilities Advocacy Program
P.O. Drawer 870395
Tuscaloosa, AL 35487-2847
205/348-4928; 800-826-1675

Director
Rehabilitation & Crippled Children Service
P.O. Box 11586
2129 E. South Blvd.
Montgomery, AL 36111-0586
205/281-8780

Special Education Action Committee
P.O. Box 161274
Mobile, AL 36616
205/478-1208

Alaska

Director of Special Education
Office of Special Services
Alaska Department of Education
P.O. Box F
Juneau, AK 99811-0500
907/465-2970

Director
Advocacy Services of Alaska
615 E. 82nd St., Suite 100
Anchorage, AK 99518
907/344-1002

Director
Division of Vocational Rehabilitation
Pouch F, MS 0581
Juneau, AK 99811
907/465-2814

American Samoa

Director of Special Education
Special Education
Department of Education
Pago Pago, American Samoa 96799
684/633-1323

Client Assistance Program
P.O. Box 3407
Pago Pago, American Samoa 96799
4-011-684-633-2418

Arizona

Director of Special Education
Special Education Section
Department of Education
1535 W. Jefferson
Phoenix, AZ 85007-3280
602/542-3184

Protection & Advocacy
Arizona Center for Law in the Public Interest
363 N. First Ave., Suite 100
Phoenix, AZ 85003
602/252-4904

Administrator
Rehabilitative Services Administration
1300 W. Washington St.
Phoenix, AZ 85007
602/255-3332

Pilot Parents
2150 E. Highland Ave.
Phoenix, AZ 85016
602/468-3001

Arkansas

Director of Special Education
Special Education Section
Arkansas Department of Education
Education Bldg., Room 105-C
#4 Capitol Mall
Little Rock, AR 72201
501/371-2161; 501/682-4214

Executive Director
Advocacy Services, Inc.
Medical Arts Bldg., Suite 311
12th and Marshall Streets
Little Rock, AR 72202
501/324-9215; 800-482-1174

Commissioner
Arkansas Department of Human Services
Rehabilitation Services Division
P.O. Box 3781
Little Rock, AR 72203

Arkansas Disability Coalition
10002 W. Markham, Suite B7
Little Rock, AR 72205
501/221-1330

FOCUS
2917 King Street, Suite C
Jonesboro, AR 72401
501/935-2750

California

Director of Special Education
Specialized Programs Branch
Special Education Division
P.O. Box 271
Sacramento, CA 95802-0271
916/445-9420

Executive Director
Protection & Advocacy, Inc.
2131 Capitol Avenue, Suite 100
Sacramento, CA 95816
916/447-3327
213/481-7431
415/839-0811
800/952-5746

Director
Department of Rehabilitation
830 K St. Mall
Sacramento, CA 95814
916/445-3971

Team of Advocates for Special Kids (TASK)
100 W. Cerritos Ave.
Annaheim, CA 92805
714/533-8275

Parents Helping Parents
535 Race Street, Suite 220
San Jose, CA 95126
408/288-5010

DREDF
2212 6th Street
Berkeley, CA 94710
415/644-2555

Disability Services Matrix
P.O. Box 6541
San Rafael, CA 94903
415/499-3877

Colorado

Director of Special Education
Special Education Services Unit
Colorado Department of Education
201 E. Colfax
Denver, CO 90203
303/866-6694

Executive Director
The Legal Center
455 Sherman Street, Suite 130
Denver, CO 80203
303/722-0300; 800-288-1376

Director
Division of Rehabilitation
Department of Social Services
1575 Sherman St., 4th Floor
Denver, CO 80203

Parent Education and Assistance for Kids (PEAK)
6055 Lehman Drive, Suite 101
Colorado Springs, CO 80918
719/531-9400
800/621-8386, Ex. 338 (in Colorado)

Connecticut

Director of Special Education
Bureau of Special Education and Pupil Personnel
    Services
25 Industrial Park
Middletown, CT 06457
203/632-1485; 800-842-8678

Executive Director
Office of Protection & Advocacy for Handicapped &
    Developmentally Disabled Persons
60B Weston St.
Hartford, CT 06120
203/297-4300
800/842-7303 (in Connecticut)

Associate Commissioner
State Department of Education
Division of Vocational Rehabilitation
600 Asylum Ave.
Hartford, CT 06105
203/566-4440

Connecticut Parent Advocacy Center, Inc.
P.O. Box 579
East Lyme, CT 06333
203/739-3089
800/445-CPAC (in Connecticut)

Delaware

Director of Special Education
Exceptional Children/Special Programs Division
Department of Public Instruction
P.O. Box 1402
Dover, DE 19903
302/736-5471

Administrator
Disabilities Law Program
913 Washington St.
Wilmington, DE 19801
800-462-7070; 800-292-7980

Director
Division of Vocational Rehabilitation
Department of Labor
State Office Building, 7th Floor
820 N. French St.
Wilmington, DE 19801
302/571-2850

Parent Information Center of Delaware, Inc.
700 Barksdale Rd., Suite 6
Newark, DE 19711
302/366-0152

District of Columbia

Director of Special Education
Division of Special Education and Pupil Personnel
    Services
D.C. Public Schools
Logan School
3rd & G St., NE
Washington, D.C. 20002
202/724-4800

Executive Director
Information, Protection, and Advocacy Center for
    Handicapped Individuals, Inc.
300 Eye St., NE, Suite 202
Washington, D.C. 20002
202/547-8081

Administrator
D.C. Rehabilitation Services Administration
Commission on Social Services
Department of Human Services
605 G St., NW, Room 1101
Washington, D.C. 20001
202/727-3227

Florida

Director of Special Education
Bureau of Education for Exceptional Studies
Florida Department of Education
Knott Building
Tallahassee, FL 32301
904/488-1570

Executive Director
Advocacy Center for Persons with Disabilities, Inc.
2661 Executive Center Circle, W
209 Clifton Bldg.
Tallahassee, FL 32301
904/488-9070
800/342-0823 Voice/TDD

Director
Division of Vocational Rehabilitation
1709-A Mahan Dr.
Tallahassee, FL 32399-0696
904/488-6210

Parent Education Network of Florida, Inc.
1211 Tech Blvd., Suite 105
Tampa, FL 33619
813/623-4088

Georgia

Director of Special Education
Program for Exceptional Children
Georgia Department of Education
1970 Twin Towers East
205 Butler Street
Atlanta, GA 30334-1601
404/656-2425

Executive Director
Georgia Advocacy Office, Inc.
1708 Peachtree St., NW, Suite 505
Atlanta, GA 30309
404/885-1234
800/282-4538 (in Georgia)

Director
Division of Rehabilitative Services
Department of Human Services
878 Peachtree St., NE, Room 706
Atlanta, GA 30309
404/894-6670

Parents Educating Parents
Georgia ARC
1851 Ram Runway, Suite 104
College Park, GA 30337
404/761-2745

Guam

Director of Special Education
Special Education
Department of Education
P.O. Box DE
Agana, Guam 97910
671/472-8901, ex. 375

Administrator
The Advocacy Office
P.O. Box 8830
Tamuning, Guam 96911
671/646-9026/27 or 646-6204

Director
Department of Vocational Rehabilitation
414 W. Soledad Ave.
Government of Guam
Agana, Guam 97910
472-8806 (Dial 011671 first)

Hawaii

Director of Special Education
Special Needs Branch
State Department of Education
3430 Leahi Avenue
Honolulu, HI 96815
808/737-3720

Executive Director
Protection & Advocacy Agency of Hawaii
1580 Makaloa St., Suite 1060
Honolulu, HI 96814
808/949-2922

Administrator
Division of Vocational Rehabilitation & Services for the
    Blind
Department of Social Services
P.O. Box 339
Honolulu, HI 96809
808/548-4769

HACLD
200 N. Vineyard Blvd., Suite 103
Honolulu, HI 96817
808/536-9684

Idaho

Director of Special Education
Special Education
State Department of Education
650 W. State Street
Boise, ID 83720-0001
208/334-3940

Idaho's Coalition of Advocates for the Disabled, Inc.
1409 W. Washington
Boise, ID 83702
208/336-5353

Administrator
Division of Vocational Rehabilitation
Len B. Jordan Bldg., Room 150
650 West State
Boise, ID 83720
208/334-3390

Idaho Parents Unltd., Inc.
1365 No. Orchard, #107
Boise, ID 83706
208/377-8049

Illinois

Director of Special Education
Illinois State Board of Education
Mail Code E-216
100 North First Street
Springfield, IL 62777-0001
217/782-6601

Director
Protection & Advocacy, Inc.
175 W. Jackson, Suite A-2103
Chicago, IL 60604
312/341-0022 Voice/TDD
800-537-2632

Director
Department of Rehabilitation Services (Illinois)
623 E. Adams St.
P.O. Box 19429
Springfield, IL 62794-9429
217/785-0218

Coordinating Council for Handicapped Children
20 E. Jackson Blvd., Room 900
Chicago, IL 60604
312/939-3513

Designs for Change
220 South State Street, Room 1900
Chicago, IL 60604
312/922-0317

Indiana

Director of Special Education
Division of Special Education
Indiana Department of Education
229 State House
Indianapolis, IN 46204
317/232-0570

Indiana Protection & Advocacy
Service Commission for the Developmentally Disabled
850 N. Meridan St. Suite 2-C
Indianapolis, IN 46204
317/232-1150
800/622-4845 (in Indiana)

Commissioner
Indiana Department of Human Services
251 N. Illinois St.
P.O. Box 7083
Indianapolis, NO 46207-7083
317/232-7000

Task Force on Education for the Handicapped, Inc.
833 Northside Blvd., Building #1–Rear
South Bend, IN 46617
219/234-7101; 800/332-4433

Iowa

Director of Special Education
Division of Special Education
Iowa Department of Public Instruction
Grimes State Office Building
Des Moines, IA 50319-0146
515/281-3176

Director
Iowa Protection & Advocacy Services, Inc.
3015 Merle Hay Rd., Suite 6
Des Moines, IA 50310
515/278-2502

Administrator
Division of Vocational Rehabilitation Services
Department of Education
510 E. 12th St.
Des Moines, IA 50319
515/281-4311

Iowa Exceptional Parent Center
33 North 12th Street
P.O. Box 1151
Ft. Dodge, IA 50501
515/576-5870

Kansas

Director of Special Education
Kansas Department of Education
120 E. Tenth Street
Topeka, KS 66612
913/296-4945

Executive Director
Kansas Advocacy & Protection Services
513 Leavenworth, Suite 2
Manhattan, KS 66502
913/776-1541
800/432-8276 (in Kansas)

Commissioner of Rehabilitation Services
Department of Social & Rehabilitative Services
Biddle Bldg., 2nd Floor
2700 W. 6th
Topeka, KS 66606
913/296-3911

Families Together, Inc.
P.O. Box 86153
Topeka, KS 66686
913/273-6343

Kentucky

Director of Special Education
Kentucky Department of Education
Office of Education for Exceptional Children
Capitol Plaza Tower, Room 820
Frankfort, KY 40601
501/564-4970

Director
Department of Public Advocacy
Protection & Advocacy Division
1274 Louisville Rd.
Perimeter Park West
Frankfort, KY 40601
502/564-2967
800/372-2988 Voice/TDD

Assistant Superintendent of Rehabilitation
Department of Education
Bureau of Rehabilitative Services
Capital Plaza Office Tower
Frankfort, KY 40601
502/564-4440

Kentucky Special Parent Involvement Network
318 W. Kentucky Street
Louisville, KY 40203
502/589-5717 or 584-1104
800/525-7746

Louisiana

Director of Special Education
Louisiana Department of Education
Special Education Services
P.O. Box 44064, 9th Floor
Baton Rouge, LA 70804-9064
504/342-3633

Executive Director
Advocate Center for the Elderly & Disabled
210 O'Keefe Ave., Suite 700
New Orleans, LA 70112
504/522-2337
800/662-7705 (in Louisiana)

Director
Division of Rehabilitation Services
P.O. Box 94371
Baton Rouge, LA 70804
504/342-2285

Project PROMPT
United Cerebral Palsy of Greater New Orleans
1500 Edwards Avenue, Suite O
Harahan, LA 70123
504/734-7736

Maine

Director of Special Education
Division of Special Education
Maine Department of Education
Station #23
Augusta, ME 04333
207/289-5953; 289-5951

Director
Main Advocacy Service
1 Grandview Pl., Suite 1
P.O. Box 445
Winthrop, ME 04364
207/377-6202; 800/452-1948

Director
Bureau of Rehabilitative Services
Department of Health & Welfare
32 Winthrop St.
Augusta, ME 04330
207/289-2266

Special Needs Parent Information Network (SPIN)
P.O.. Box 2067
Augusta, ME 04338-2067
207/582-2504
800/325-0220 (in Maine)

Maryland

Director of Special Education
Division of Special Education
Maryland State Department of Education
200 W. Baltimore Street
Baltimore, MD 21201-2595
301/333-2489

Director
Maryland Disability Law Center
2510 St. Paul St.
Baltimore, MD 21218
301/333-7600

Assistant State Superintendent
Division of Vocational Rehabilitation
State Department of Education
200 W. Baltimore St.
Baltimore, MD 21201
301/659-2294

See Parent Educational Advocacy Training Center
 Under Virginia

Massachusetts

Director of Special Education
Division of Special Education
Massachusetts Department of Education
1385 Hancock Street, 3rd Floor
Quincy, MA 02169
617/770-7468

Executive Director
DD Law Center of Massachusetts
11 Beacon Street, Suite 925
Boston, MA 02108
617/723-8455

Commissioner
Massachusetts Rehabilitation Commission
20 Park Plaza, 11th Floor
Boston, MA 02116
617/727-2172

Federation for Children with Special Needs
95 Berkeley St., Suite 104
Boston, MA 02116
617/482-2915
800/331-0688 (in Massachusetts)

Michigan

Director of Special Education
Special Education Services
Michigan Department of Education
P.O. Box 30008
Lansing, MI 48909-7508
517/373-9433

Executive Director
Michigan Protection & Advocacy Service, Inc.
109 W. Michigan Ave., Suite 900
Lansing, MI 48933
517/487-1755

State Director
Michigan Rehabilitation Services
Michigan Department of Education
P.O. Box 30010
Lansing, MI 48909
517/373-0683

United Cerebral Palsy Assn. of Metropolitan Detroit
Parents Training Parents Project
17000 West 8 Mile Road, Suite 380
Southfield, MI 48075
313/557-5070

Citizens Alliance to Uphold Special Education (CAUSE)
313 South Washington Sq., Suite 040
Lansing, MI 48933
517/485-4084
800/221-9105 (in Michigan)

Minnesota

Director of Special Education
Special Education Section
Department of Education
812 Capitol Square Bldg.
550 Cedar Street
St. Paul, MN 55101-2233
612/359-3490

Legal Advocacy–Disability Law Center
222 Grain Exchange Bldg.
323 Fourth Ave., S.
Minneapolis, MN 55415
612/338-0968; 332-1441
800-292-4150

Assistant Commissioner
Division of Rehabilitation Services
Department of Jobs and Training
390 N. Robert St., 5th Floor
St. Paul, MN 55101
612/296-1822

PACER Center, Inc.
4826 Chicago Avenue South
Minneapolis, MN 55417
612/827-2966
800/53-PACER (in Minnesota)

Mississippi

Director of Special Education
Bureau of Special Services
State Department of Education
P.O. Box 771
Jackson, MS 39205-0771
601/359-3490

Executive Director
Mississippi Protection & Advocacy System, Inc.
4793B McWillie Dr.
Jackson, MS 39206
601/981-8207
800/772-4057 (in Mississippi)

Director
Department of Rehabilitation Services
Vocational Rehabilitation Division
932 N. State St.
P.O. Box 1698
Jackson, MS 39215-1698
601/354-6825

Association of Developmental Organizations of Mississippi
322 New Market Dr.
Jackson, MS 39209
601/922-3210
800/231-3721 (in Mississippi)

Missouri

Director of Special Education
Special Education
Department of Elementary and Secondary Education
P.O. Box 480
Jefferson City, MO 65102
314/751-2965; 751-4212

Missouri Protection & Advocacy Services
925 S. Country Club Dr.
Jefferson City, MO 65101
314/893-3333
800/392-8667 (in Missouri)

Assistant Commissioner
State Department of Education
Division of Vocational Rehabilitation
2401 E. McCarty
Jefferson City, MO 65101
314/751-3251

Missouri Parents Act (MPACT)
625 N. Euclid, Suite 225
St. Louis, MO 63108
314/361-1660; 800/284-6389

MPACT
1722 S. Glenstone, Suite 125
Springfield, MO 65804
417/882-7434; 800/666-7228

Montana

Director of Special Education
Special Education
Office of Public Instruction
State Capitol, Room 106
Helena, MT 59620
406/444-4429

Executive Director
Montana Advocacy Program
1410 8th Avenue
Helena, MT 59601
406/444-3889
800/245-4743 (in Montana)

Administrator
Department of Social & Rehabilitative Services
Rehabilitative-Visual Services Division
P.O. Box 4210
Helena, MT 59604
406/444-2590

Parents, Let's Unite for Kids (PLUK)
1500 N. 30th Street
Billings, MT 59101
406/657-2055
800/222-PLUK (in Montana)

Nebraska

Director of Special Education
Special Education
Nebraska Department of Education
Box 94987
Lincoln, NE 68509-4987
402/471-2471

Executive Director
Nebraska Advocacy Services, Inc.
522 Lincoln Center Bldg.
215 Centennial Mall South
Lincoln, NE 68508
402/474-3183
800/422-6691 (in Nebraska)

Associate Commissioner & Director
Division of Rehabilitative Services
State Department of Education
301 Centennial Mall, 6th Floor
Lincoln, NE 68509
402/471-2961

Nebraska Parent Information Training Center
3610 Dodge St., Suite 102
Omaha, NE 68131
402/346-0525

Nevada

Director of Special Education
Special Education
Nevada Department of Education
Capitol Complex
400 W. King Street
Carson City, NV 89710-0004
702/885-3140

Project Director
Office of Protection & Advocacy
6122 W. Charleston
Las Vegas, NV 89102
702/486-7600

Administrator, Rehabilitation Division
Department of Human Resources
Kinkead Bldg., 5th Floor
505 E. King St.
Carson City, NV 89710
702/885-4440

Nevada Association for the Handicapped
6200 W. Oakey Blvd.
Las Vegas, NV 89102-1142
702/870-7050

New Hampshire

Director of Special Education
Special Education Bureau
New Hampshire Department of Education
101 Pleasant Street
Concord, NH 03301-3860
603/271-3741

Executive Director
Disabilities Rights Center, Inc.
94 Washington St.
P.O. Box 19
Concord, NH 03302-0019
603/228-0432

Director
State Department of Education
Division of Vocational Rehabilitation
78 Regional Dr., Bldg. JB
Concord, NH 03301
603/271-3471

Parent Information Center
151A Manchester St.
P.O. Box 1422
Concord, NH 03302-1422
603/224-6299

New Jersey

Director of Special Education
Division of Special Education
New Jersey Department of Education
P.O. Box CN 500
225 W. State St.
Trenton, NJ 08625-0001
609/292-0147

Director
Division of Advocacy for the Developmentally Disabled
Hughes Justice Complex, CN850
Trenton, NJ 08625
609/292-9742
800/792-8600 (in New Jersey)

Director, Division of Vocational Rehabilitation Services
Labor & Industry Bldg., CN398
John Fitch Plaza, Rm. 1005
Trenton, NJ 08625
609/292-5987

Statewide Parent Advocacy Network (SPAN)
516 North Avenue East
Westfield, NJ 07090
201/654-7726

New Mexico

Director of Special Education
Special Education
State Department of Education
State Educational Building
Santa Fe, NM 87501-2786
505/827-6541

Protection & Advocacy System
1720 Louisiana NE, Suite 204
Albuquerque, NM 87110
505/256-3100
800/432-4682 (in New Mexico)

DVR Director
Division of Vocational Rehabilitation
604 W. San Mateo
Santa Fe, NM 87503
505/827-3511

Education for Indian Children with Special Needs
    (EPICS)
P.O. Box 788
Bernalillo, NM 87004
505/867-3396

Parents Reaching Out to Help
1127 University NE
Albuquerque, NM 87102
505/842-9045
800/524-5176

New York

Director of Special Education
New York State Department of Education
Office of Education of Children with Handicapping
    Conditions
Education Building Annex, Room 1073
Albany, NY 12234-0001
518/474-5548

Commissioner
New York Commission on Quality of Care for the
    Mentally Disabled
99 Washington Ave., Suite 1002
Albany, NY 12210
518/473-4057

Deputy Director
Office of Vocational Rehabilitation
One Commerce Plaza, Room 1907
Albany, NY 12234
518/474-2714

Advocates for Children of New York City
24-16 Bridge Plaza South
Long Island City, NY 11101
718/729-8866

Parent Network Center
1443 Main Street
Buffalo, NY 14209
716/885-1004

North Carolina

Director of Special Education
Division of Exceptional Children
North Carolina State Department of Public Instruction
    Education Bldg., Room 442
116 W. Edenton
Raleigh, NC 27603-1712
919/733-3921

Director
Governor's Advocacy Council for Persons with Disabili-
    ties
1318 Dale St., Suite 100
Raleigh, NC 27605
919/733-9250
800/821-6922

Director
Division of Vocational Rehabilitation Services
Department of Human Resources
State Office
P.O. Box 26053
Raleigh, NC 27611
919/733-3364

Exceptional Children's Assistance Center
P.O. Box 16
Davidson, NC 28036
704/892-1321

North Dakota

Director of Special Education
Special Education
Department of Public Instruction
State Capitol, 600 E. Blvd. Ave.
Bismarck, ND 58505-0440
701/224-2277

Director
Protection & Advocacy Project
400 E. Broadway, Suite 515
Bismarck, ND 58501
701/224-2950
800/472-2670 (in North Dakota)

Division Director
Division of Vocational Rehabilitation
State Capitol Bldg.
Bismarck, ND 58505
701/224-2907

Pathfinder Services of North Dakota
16th St. & 2nd Ave., SW
Arrowhead Shopping Center
Minot, ND 58701
701/852-9426

Ohio

Director of Special Education
Ohio Department of Education
Division of Special Education
933 High Street
Worthington, Oh 43085-4017
614/466-2650

Executive Director
Ohio Legal Rights Services
8 E. Long St., 5th Floor
Columbus, OH 43215
800/282-9181 (in Ohio)

Administrator
Ohio Rehabilitation Services Commission
4656 Heaton Rd.
Columbus, OH 43229
614/438-1210

Child Advocacy Center
106 Wellington Place, Suite LL
Cincinnati, OH 45219
513/381-2400

Ohio Coalition for the Education of Handicapped
    Children
1299 Campbell Rd., Suite B
Marion, OH 43302

Oklahoma

Director of Special Education
Special Education Section
State Department of Education
Oliver Hodge Memorial Bldg.
2500 N. Lincoln, Room 215
Oklahoma City, OK 73105-4599
405/521-3352

Director
Protection & Advocacy Agency
9726 E. 42nd Street
Osage Bldg., Suite 133
Tulsa, OK 74146
918/664-5883

Administrator of Rehabilitation Services
Department of Human Services
23rd & Lincoln, Sequoyah Bldg.
P.O. Box 25352
Oklahoma City, OK 73125
405/521-3646

PRO-Oklahoma (Parents Reaching Out in Oklahoma)
1917 S. Harvard Avenue
Oklahoma City, OK 73128
405/681-9710
800/PL94-142

Oregon

Director of Special Education
Special Education and Student Services Division
Oregon Department of Education
700 Pringle Parkway, S.E.
Salem, OR 97310-0290
503/378-3598

Executive Director
Oregon Developmental Disabilities Advocacy Center
625 Board of Trade Bldg.
310 S.W. 4th Avenue
Portland, OR 97204
503/243-2081

Administrator
Division of Vocational Rehabilitation
Department of Human Resources
2045 Silverton Rd., NE
Salem, OR 97310
503/378-3830

Oregon Coalition for Exceptional Children and Young
    Adults/COPE
Oregon COPE Project
999 Locust Street, NE, Box B
Salem, OR 97303
503/373-7477

Pennsylvania

Director of Special Education
Bureau of Special Education
Pennsylvania Department of Education
333 Market Street
Harrisburg, PA 17126-0333
717/783-6913

Pennsylvania Protection & Advocacy, Inc.
116 Pine St., Suite 102
Harrisburg, PA 17101
717/236-8110
800/692-7443 (in Pennsylvania)

Executive Director
Office of Vocational Rehabilitation
Labor & Industry Bldg.
Seventh & Forster Streets
Harrisburg, PA 17120
717/787-5244

Mentor Parent Program
Route 257, Salina Road
P.O. Box 718
Seneca, PA 16346
814/676-8615
800/447-1431

Parents Union for Public Schools
311 S. Juniper St., Suite 602
Philadelphia, PA 19107
215/546-1212

Parent Education Network
240 Haymeadow Drive
York, PA 17402
717/845-9722

Puerto Rico

Director of Special Education
Special Education
Department of Education
G.P.O. Box 759
Hato Rey, PR 00919-0759
809/764-8059

Director
Planning Research and Special Projects
Ombudsman for the Disabled
Governor's Office
Chardon Ave., #916
Hato Rey, PR 00936
809/766-2333/2388

Assistant Secretary for Vocational Rehabilitation
Department of Social Services
P.O. Box 118
Hato Rey, PR 00919
809/725-1792

Associacion Padres Pro Bienestar/Ninos
    Impedidos de Puerto Rico
P.O. Box 21301
Rio Piedras, PR 00928
809/765-0345/763-4665

Rhode Island

Director of Special Education
Special Education Program Services Unit
R.I. Department of Education
Roger Williams Bldg., Room 209
22 Hayes Street
Providence, RI 02908-5025
401/277-3505

Executive Director
Rhode Island Protection & Advocacy System
55 Bradford St.
Providence, RI 02903
401/831-3150 Voice/TDD

Administrator, Vocational Rehabilitation
Division of Community Services
Department of Human Services
40 Fountain St.
Providence, RI 02903
401/421-7005 (TDD 421-7016)

South Carolina

Director of Special Education
Office of Programs for Handicapped
South Carolina Department of Education
100 Executive Center Drive, A-24
Columbia, SC 29201
803/737-8710

Executive Director
South Carolina Protection & Advocacy System for the
    Handicapped, Inc.
2360-A Two Notch Road
Columbia, SC 29204
803/782-0639

Commissioner
South Carolina Vocational Rehabilitation Department
P.O. Box 15
W. Columbia, SC 29171-0015
803/734-4300

South Dakota

Director of Special Education
Section for Special Education
State of South Dakota Department of Education
700 Governor's Drive
Pierre, SD 57501
605/773-3678

Executive Director
South Dakota Advocacy Project, Inc.
221 S. Central Ave.
Pierre, SD 57501
605/224-8294
800/742-8108 (in South Dakota)

Secretary
Division of Rehabilitative Services
Department of Vocational Rehabilitation
State Office Bldg.
700 Governors Dr.
Pierre, SD 57501
605/773-3195

South Dakota Parent Connection
P.O. Box 84813
Sioux Falls, SD 57118-4813
605/335-8844
800/640-4553 (in South Dakota)

Tennessee

Director of Special Education
Special Programs
State of Tennessee Department of Education
132 Cordell Hull Bldg.
Nashville, TN 37243
615/741-2851

Director
E.A.C.H., Inc.
P.O. Box 121257
Nashville, TN 37212
615/298-1080
1-800-342-1660 (in Tennessee)
Voice/TTY

Assistant Commissioner
Division of Rehabilitation Services
1808 W. End Bldg., Room 900
Nashville, TN 37203
615/741-2095

STEP
1805 Hayes St., Suite 100
Nashville, TN 37203
615/327-0294

Texas

Director of Special Education
Special Education Programs
Texas Education Agency
1701 N. Congress Ave., Room 5-120
Austin, TX 78701-2486
512/463-9734

Executive Director
Advocacy, Inc.
7800 Shoal Creek Blvd., Suite 171E
Austin, TX 78757
512/454-4816
800/252-9108 (in Texas)

Commissioner
Texas Rehabilitation Commission
118 E. Riverside Drive
Austin, TX 78704
512/445-8100

Partnerships for Assisting Texans with Handicaps
    (PATH)
6465 Calder Ave., Suite 202
Beaumont, TX 77707
409/866-4726

Utah

Director of Special Education
Utah State Office of Education
250 E. 500 South
Salt Lake City, UT 84111
801/538-7700

Executive Director
Legal Center for the Handicapped
455 East 400 South, Suite 201
Salt Lake City, UT 84111
801/363-1347
800/662-9080 (in Utah)

Executive Director
Vocational Rehabilitation Agency
250 E. 500 South
Salt Lake City, UT 84111
801/533-5991

Utah Parent Center
2290 East 4500 South, Suite 110
Salt Lake City, UT 84117
801/272-1051
800/468-1160

Vermont

Director of Special Education
Division of Special and Compensatory Education
Vermont Department of Education
State Office Bldg.
120 State Street
Montpelier, VT 05602-3403
802/828-3141

Director
Vermont DD Protection and Advocacy, Inc.
12 North St.
P.O. Box 1367
Burlington, VT 05401
802/863-2881

Director
Vocational Rehabilitation Division
Osgood Bldg., Waterbury Complex
103 S. Main St.
Waterbury, VT 05676
802/241-2189

Vermont Association for Retarded Citizens
Information and Training Network
37 Champlain Mill
Winooski, VT 05404
802/655-4016

Virgin Islands

Director of Special Education
Department of Education
State Office of Special Education
P.O. Box 6640
Charlotte Amalie, St. Thomas
Virgin Islands 00801
809/774-4399

Director
Committee on Advocacy for the Developmentally
    Disabled, Inc.
31-A New Street, Apt. No. 2
Fredericksted, St. Croix
U.S. Virgin Islands 00840
809/722-1200

Administrator
Division of Disabilities & Rehabilitation Services
Department of Human Services
Barbel Plaza South
St. Thomas, VI 00801
809/774-0930

Virginia

Office of Special and Compensatory Education
Virginia Department of Education
P.O. Box 6Q
Richmond, VA 23216-2060
804/225-2880

Director
Department of Rights for the Disabled
James Monroe Bldg.
101 N. 14th St., 17th Floor
Richmond, VA 23219
804/225-2042
800/552-3962 (in Virginia)

Commissioner
Department of Rehabilitation Services
Commonwealth of Virginia
P.O. Box 11045
4901 Fitzhugh Ave.
Richmond, VA 23230
804/367-0316

Parent Educational Advocacy Training Center
228 S. Pitt St., Suite 300
Alexandria, VA 22314
703/836-2953
(Serves Virginia, Maryland, and West Virginia)

Virginia Parent Resource Centers–State Team
Department of Education
P.O. Box 6Q
Richmond, VA 23216-2060
804/371-7581
804/225-2869

Washington

Director of Special Education
Special Education Section
Superintendent of Public Instruction
Old Capital Bldg.
Olymphia, WA 98502-0001
206/753-6733

Washington Protection & Advocacy System
1550 W. Armory Way, Suite 204
Seattle, WA 98119
800/562-2702 (in Washington)

Director, Division of Vocational Rehabilitation
State Office Bldg., No. 2
Department of Social & Health Services
P.O. Box 1788 (MS 21-C)
Olympia, WA 98504
206/753-0293

Washington PAVE
6316 South 12th South
Tacoma, WA 98465
206/565-2266 Voice/TDD
800/5-PARENT (in Washington)

West Virginia

Director of Special Education
Special Education
West Virginia Department of Education
Bldg. #6, Room B-304
Charleston, WV 25305
304/348-2696

Executive Director
West Virginia Advocates for the Developmentally
    Disabled, Inc.
1524 Kanawha Blvd. East
Charleston, WV 25311
304/346-0847
800/950-5250 (in West Virginia)

Director
Division of Rehabilitation Services
West Virginia State Board of Rehabilitation
State Capitol Bldg.
Charleston, WV 25305

See Parent Educational Advocacy Training Center
   under Virginia

Wisconsin

Director of Special Education
Division of Handicapped Children and Pupil Services
Department of Public Instruction
125 S. Webster
P.O. Box 7841
Madison, WI 53707
608/266-1649

Executive Director
Wisconsin Coalition for Advocacy, Inc.
16 N. Carroll, Suite 400
Madison, WI 53703
608/267-0214

Administrator
Division of Vocational Rehabilitation
Department of Health & Social Services
1 Wilson St., Room 850
P.O. Box 7852
Madison, WI 53702
608/266-5466

Parent Education Project
United Cerebral Palsy of SE Wisconsin
230 W. Wells Street, Suite 502
Milwaukee, WI 53203
414/272-4500

Wyoming

Director of Special Education
State Department of Education
Hathaway Bldg., 2nd Floor
2300 Capitol Avenue
Cheyenne, WY 82002-0050
307/777-7417

Executive Director
Protection & Advocacy System, Inc.
2424 Pioneer Ave., No. 101
Cheyenne, WY 82001
307/632-3496
800/624-3496 (in Wyoming)

Administrator
Division of Vocational Rehabilitation
Department of Health & Social Services
326 Hathaway Bldg.
Cheyenne, WY 82002
307/777-7385

Indian Affairs

Director of Special Education
Bureau of Exceptional Education
Office of Indian Education Program
Bureau of Indian Affairs
18th & C Streets, NW, Room 4642
Washington, DC 20245
202/343-6675

Appendix D

Sample IEP Form

The following pages include a sample IEP Form. As noted in the description of an IEP on pp. 45–46, state and federal regulations stipulate that every IEP must include certain provisions. However, each school division may develop its own form.

The IEP which follows is an example of the format used by Chesterfield County Public Schools in Virginia and is reproduced here with their permission. It may be helpful to review this form while referring to pp. 45–46, which delineates the required provisions of an IEP.

Prior to an IEP meeting for your child, you may want to request a **blank** copy of the form used by your school division so that you can familiarize yourself with the particular format used.

CHESTERFIELD COUNTY PUBLIC SCHOOLS INDIVIDUALIZED EDUCATION PROGRAM

CONFIDENTIAL INFORMATION

School Year 199____ - 199____

Name: _____ S.S. #: ____-__-____ DOB: __/__/__ Age: _____ School: _____ Grade: _____

Date of IEP Meeting: __/__/__ Initial Eligibility: __/__/__ Most Recent Eligibility/Triennial: __/__/__ Next Triennial Due By: __/__/__

Parent Notification of IEP Meeting: (1) Goal Setting Worksheet Sent __/__/__ (2) __:__ (3) __/__/__ : __/__/__

This IEP will be in effect from __/__/__ to __/__/__ Disability - (From SE 5) _____

Current Level of Educational Performance:

SERVICES PROVIDED IN: Special Education & Related Services	Hours/Day	Times/Week	Projected Initiation/Duration	Location and/or Provider of Service	PARTICIPATION IN: General/Vocational Education or Non-Academic Activities	Hours/Day	Times/Week

Adapted Physical Education _____ Physical Education

Does the program described above ensure 5 1/2 hours of instruction per day? Yes _____ No _____ If no, state reason

Transportation: Regular: _____ Special (accommodations needed): _____

CHESTERFIELD COUNTY PUBLIC SCHOOLS INDIVIDUALIZED EDUCATIONAL PROGRAM

Student Name _____

School Year 199___ - 199___

IEP PARTICIPANTS:

Your signature below indicates that you have had the opportunity to participate in the development of the IEP.

Signature of Participants	Position	Date Signed
_____	Parent/Legal Guardian	___/___/___
_____	Administrator/Designee	___/___/___
_____	Teacher	___/___/___
_____		___/___/___
_____		___/___/___
_____		___/___/___
_____		___/___/___
_____		___/___/___

CONTINUUM OF PLACEMENT OPTIONS

Number 1 is the least restrictive and number 10 is the most restrictive. After considering all options below, select the appropriate placement. Provide a written justification for the placement chosen. Include why less restrictive placements are not appropriate.

1. ___ Direct instruction and/or consultative services within general/vocational education
2. ___ Direct instruction and/or consultative services within general/vocational education with additional instruction in a resource room
3. ___ General/vocational education with content instruction in one or more special education classes
4. ___ Self-contained class with integration as appropriate
5. ___ Self-contained class with no integration in regular public school
6. ___ Separate public day school
7. ___ Private day school for students with disabilities
8. ___ Public and/or private residential facility
9. ___ Homebound
10. ___ Hospital
11. ___ Other (including preschool options) _____

JUSTIFICATION: _____
_____
_____

PARENTAL AUTHORIZATION FOR SPECIAL EDUCATION PROGRAM

___ I give permission for my child to be enrolled in the special education program described in this Individualized Education Program.

Signature of Parent(s)/Guardian(s) _____ Month ___ Day ___ Year ___

___ I do not give permission for my child to be enrolled in the special education program described in this Individualized Education Program. I understand that I have the right to refuse this placement and to have my child continue in his/her present placement pending exhaustion of my due process rights.

Signature of Parent(s)/Guardian(s) _____ Month ___ Day ___ Year ___

Reason(s)/Comment(s) _____
_____

___ I have received a copy of this IEP. (Please Initial).

TERMINATION OF SERVICES STATEMENT

___ I give permission for the termination of _____ services for my child.

___ I do not give permission for the termination of _____ services for my child.

Signature of Parent(s)/Guardian(s) _____ Month ___ Day ___ Year ___

___ I request termination of _____ services for my child.

Signature of Parent(s)/Guardian(s) _____ Month ___ Day ___ Year ___

Confidential Permanent Record: Do Not Destroy   White: Confidential Copy   Yellow: Parent Copy

AAA-1216
SE 10-3 (2/91)

CHESTERFIELD COUNTY PUBLIC SCHOOLS
Individualized Education Program

Student Name _____

School Year 199 _____ -199 _____

During this school year, the student will participate in:

	Yes		No	Attach a copy of the Family Life Education Opt-Out form, if appropriate
Family Life Education:	☐ Yes	☐ No		
VA State Assessment Program:	☐ Yes	☐ No Accommodations	☐ With Accommodations (see below)	
		☐ Test Not Administered at this grade	Other Reasons: _____	
Literacy Test Program:	☐ Yes	☐ No Accommodations	☐ With Accommodations (see below)	
		☐ No Test Not Administered at this grade	Other Reasons: _____	

For High School Students Only (to be initially completed at 9th grade IEP meeting and reviewed annually)
This student is a candidate for: High School Diploma ☐   Special Education Certificate ☐   GED Certificate ☐
Anticipated date of Graduation: _____ Special Education services end upon receiving a high school diploma, special education certificate, or GED certificate.

Testing Procedure Accommodations

Students with disabilities may need accommodations to regular testing procedures in order to demonstrate achievement. Accommodations needed must have a direct relationship to the student's disability. These accommodations may include alternative test formats, aids, and personalized testing environments. Some accommodations used in the student's regular instructional program may be used during the Virginia State Assessment Program and the Literacy Test Program. No accommodations should be used in the Virginia State Assessment Program or the Literacy Test Program that are not used in the student's regular instructional program. Consult directions for each test to be certain specific accommodations are permitted.

☐ The student will not need accommodations during test administration within the regular instructional program.
☐ The student will need the following accommodations during test administration within the regular instructional program.

Accommodations in Test Format

☐ *Audio-Cassette
☐ Braille
☐ Large-Print
☐ *Oral Administration
☐ †Write in Test Booklet
☐ †Sign Language Interpretation
☐ Other: _____

Accommodations by Use of Aids

☐ Answers Recorded by Proctor
☐ Braille-Writer
☐ Abacus
☐ *Dictation to a Scribe
☐ Dictation into a Tape Recorder
☐ *Electronic Calculators
☐ †Other calculation devices
☐ †Templates, graph paper

☐ Interpreting Test Directions
☐ Magnification
☐ Marking Responses in Test Booklet
☐ Place Keepers, Trackers, Pointers
☐ Written Directions
☐ †Noise Buffers
☐ †Electronic Speller
☐ Typewriter, Word Processor,
   Augmentative Communication
   Device
☐ Other: _____

Accommodations to Test Environment

☐ *Multiple Test Sessions
☐ Testing in a Separate Room
☐ Hospital/Home Setting
☐ Other: _____

*Designated as "Non-Standard Administration" for one or more sections of the Literacy Test Program. For such sections, this would be considered a test modification, not an accommodation. A specific notation must be attached to the test. Consult Literacy Program materials for further information.
Confidential Permanent Record: Do Not Destroy

AAA-1217
SE 10-3a (2/91)

CHESTERFIELD COUNTY PUBLIC SCHOOLS

Student Name _____

School Year 199____ -199____

Instructional Modifications

Students with disabilities may require modifications in instructional procedures and class assignments in order to demonstrate achievement. Modifications required must have a direct relationship to the identified needs of the student for special education services.

Modifications Required

Location and/or Provider(s)

CHESTERFIELD COUNTY PUBLIC SCHOOLS INDIVIDUALIZED EDUCATION PROGRAM

SE 10-2 (2/91)

Name_____ School Year 199_____ - 199_____   Page_____

ANNUAL GOAL: The student will:

SHORT TERM OBJECTIVES	Grading Period	COMMENTS
Objective:	1.	
	2.	

Evaluation:
    Criterion_____
    Frequency_____
    Procedure:
	3.	

Beginning Skill Level:		
	4.	
Date Initiated:_____/_____ Mastered:_____/_____		
Objective:	1.	
	2.	

Evaluation:
    Criterion_____
    Frequency_____
    Procedure:
	3.	

Beginning Skill Level:		
	4.	
Date Initiated:_____/_____ Mastered:_____/_____		
Objective:	1.	
	2.	

Evaluation:
    Criterion_____
    Frequency_____
    Procedure:
	3.	

Beginning Skill Level:		
	4.	
Date Initiated:_____/_____ Mastered:_____/_____		

Short term objectives will be monitored each nine weeks (unless otherwise indicated) and evaluated in comparison to each objective criterion level.

Progress Key: **No mark** - Objective not initiated   **P** - Progressing on the objective   **NC** - No change
        D - Having difficulty with the objective (comment to describe difficulty)
        M - Objective mastered   **M/R** - Objective mastered but needs review to maintain mastery

AAA-1217B
SE 10-4a
Part I
(2/91)

CHESTERFIELD COUNTY PUBLIC SCHOOLS INDIVIDUALIZED EDUCATION PROGRAM
TRANSITIONAL SERVICES AND PROVIDER GUIDE SHEET

NAME: _____

	Type of Services Needed	Service Provider	Time Frame
CONTINUING EDUCATION/POST SECONDARY EDUCATION OPTIONS			
4 Year College			
Community College			
Apprenticeship			
Trade School			
Military			
EMPLOYMENT/VOCATIONAL PLACEMENT OPTIONS			
Fulltime Employment			
Part-time Employment			
Sheltered/Supervised Employment			
Vocational Training			
Work Adjustment			
LIVING ARRANGEMENT OPTIONS			
Shared Living (roommate)			
Independent Living (by self)			
With Family			
Supervised Living			
Residential Care			
Adult Foster Care			
INCOME OPTIONS			
Self Sufficient Earning			
General Public Assistance			
Food Stamps			
Supplemental Security Income (SSI)			
Social Security Benefits			

Confidential Permanent Record: Do Not Destroy

– 125 –

CHESTERFIELD COUNTY PUBLIC SCHOOLS INDIVIDUALIZED EDUCATION PROGRAM
TRANSITIONAL SERVICES AND PROVIDER GUIDE SHEET

NAME: _____

Type of Services Needed	Service Provider	Time Frame
PERSONAL MANAGEMENT ASSISTANCE OPTIONS		
Household Management		
Management		
Employment Social Skills		
Community Social Skills		
Hygiene Skills		
Counseling/Therapy		
Behavioral		
Occupational		
Physical		
Speech/Language/Hearing		
Vision		
TRANSPORTATION OPTIONS		
Licensed Driver		
Public Transportation		
Specialized Transportation		
Driven by Parent		
MEDICAL CARE OPTIONS		
Independent Usage		
Medical		
Dental		
Specialized Usage		
Medical		
Dental		
Insurance		
Medical		
Health		
FAMILY AID OPTIONS		
Counseling		
Legal Aid Services		
Alternate Guardianship		

Confidential Permanent Record: Do Not Destroy

Appendix E

Parents' Rights

Understanding Your Rights and Responsibilities

Why should you, as a parent, go to the trouble of finding out what your rights are? Because failure to know or assert your rights becomes, in effect, a waiver of your rights as the parent of a learning disabled child. Of course, the public school system has rights too, and both school and parents have certain responsibilities, as defined by Public Law 94-142 and 101–476, Individuals with Disabilities Education Act (IDEA).

The parental rights which are outlined below are interpreted in different ways by different individuals. Also, laws frequently change. Therefore, you should be careful to determine that your position is correct **before** you assert a right.

These are your rights as a parent:

- *Pertaining To Identification of Handicap:* You have the right...

  - to request that a comprehensive assessment be conducted at no cost to you when you suspect your child is handicapped.

  - to receive notice and give (or refuse to give) consent before evaluation may take place.

  - to see the results of the evaluations and have them explained, upon request.

  - to examine all of your child's records.

  - to have your child tested in **all** areas related to the suspected disability including, where appropriate, vision, hearing, speech and language, motor and perceptual abilities, and emotional status—as well as the required tests of general intelligence, academic performance, social and medical status.

  - to request an independent evaluation at public expense if you disagree with the school division's evaluation.

  - to have the school division consider all independent evaluations in determining your child's educational needs.

  - to have the school division consider all reports from professionals independent of the school system.

  - to a complete reevaluation every three years or more frequently upon request.

- *Pertaining To Eligibility Determination:* You have the right...

  - to have eligibility for special education services be determined by a team of people including: the building principal or his designee, the supervisor of special education or his designee, the child's current teacher, and at least one person who participated in your child's evaluation. You may ask to attend and to bring someone for moral and/or technical support.

- *Pertaining To IEP Development:* You have the right...

  - to have an Individualized Educational Plan (IEP) in effect within thirty days of the date when it was determined your child was eligible for LD services.

  - to have the IEP meeting scheduled at a time which is mutually convenient for you and school personnel, and to participate in all meetings regarding the development, revision, and review of the IEP.

– to have the following written into your child's IEP:

(a) A statement of your child's present educational performance level

(b) The extent and duration of both regular and special education and related services.

(c) A statement of annual goals and short-term instructional objectives designed to achieve those goals.

(d) The dates for initiation and anticipated duration of services.

(e) Objective criteria, evaluation procedures, and schedules for determining at least annually whether instructional objectives are being achieved.

(f) For students 14 years of age and older, a statement of transition services which will help the student move successfully from school to the "real world," with a listing of those agencies, besides the school, which will provide services. The school is responsible for obtaining services from other agencies where necessary and for reconvening the IEP team to seek alternatives if another agency fails to provide the services specified.

– to related services, as appropriate, which may include special transportation, psychotherapy, speech and language therapy, physical or occupational therapy, rehabilitation counseling, social work services or assistive technology, such as computers, etc.; these are written into the IEP and are provided without cost.

– to have your child's placement, educational program, and related services specified in the IEP.

– to have an expert or someone of your choosing accompany you to the IEP meeting.

– to have an interpreter present at the meeting if you are hearing impaired or if your native language is other than English.

– to receive a copy of your child's IEP.

● *Pertaining To Placement and Service Delivery:* You have the right...

– to consent to the proposed placement before services may be delivered.

– to have your child placed in a program which is appropriate, as close as possible to your home, and delivered in the least restrictive environment.

– to request a re-evaluation after your child is placed in a program if you feel his or her condition or needs have changed.

– to receive free special education and related services regardless of family's insurance coverage. The reasons: (1) coverage or benefits may be reduced if parents file a claim; (2) insurance premiums may be increased; and/or (3) parents may be charged for filing a claim. Insurance coverage for a child and the entire family may be placed in jeopardy. (Ref: Education Daily, 1981)

– to follow and be informed of your child's progress in the program in which he or she is placed.

● *Pertaining To Records:* You have the right...

– to receive, upon request, a list of the types of records kept on your child, their location, and how you may obtain access to them.

– to inspect, review, and copy any of your child's records without unnecessary delay.

– to have someone at school explain or interpret information or material in your child's records.

– to receive copies of the records if this is the only way to insure access to them. A fee may be charged for these copies if such a charge does not effectively prevent your access to the information; however, a copy of the IEP must be provided free of charge.

– to have a representative of your choosing inspect and review the records.

– to ask the school to change or delete any statement or information contained in your child's records which you believe is incorrect or misleading. The school must either change this statement within a reasonable period of time or formally refuse. If the school refuses, school officials must inform you of their refusal and advise you of your rights to a hearing on the matter.

- to a hearing on the change you requested in the records, conducted by a school official who does not have a direct interest in its outcome. If the hearing is decided in your favor, school officials must change the information and inform you in writing that this has been done. If the hearing is decided in the school division's favor, you have the right to add a statement to the record. This addition must be kept with the records for as long as the records are kept. If your child's records are shown to anyone, this statement must also be included.

● *Pertaining to An Impartial Due Process Hearing*: You have the right...

- to request an impartial due process hearing, within six months of a disagreement, when the school division proposes to initiate or refuses to initiate or change the identification, evaluation, or the provision of a free appropriate public education for your child.

- to have present an attorney or other individuals with specialized knowledge or training; however, you also have the right to have present a lay advocate; it is not necessary to have an attorney.

- to present evidence, confront, cross-examine, and compel witnesses to attend the hearing. (The hearing officer has the authority to compel the attendance of witnesses at the request of either party.)

- to prohibit introduction of any documentary evidence or witnesses at the hearing which have not been disclosed to the other party at least five working days before the hearing.

- to request and obtain a written or electronic verbatim record of the hearing, when either party appeals the local hearing decision.

- to obtain findings of fact and decisions rendered by the hearing officer.

- to be informed by the school division of any low-cost legal and/or other relevant services available in the area when: (a) you request such information, or (b) a hearing is initiated by you or by the school.

- to have your child present at an impartial due process hearing.

- to appeal the decision of the hearing officer to a reviewing officer.

- to appeal the decision of the reviewing officer to either a U.S. District Court or the State court in your jurisdiction.

- to recover from the school system reasonable attorney's fees if the hearing officer or judge rules in your favor. Included are expenses incurred in providing competent representation, such as witness fees, medical and diagnostic expenses, and costs for transcripts, depositions, travel, etc. These fees cannot be recovered if the school system prevails in the case, or if the school division offers to settle the case ten days before the hearing and the settlement is substantially similar to the outcome. An award of fees is in the discretion of the court.

● *Additional Parent Rights:* You have the right...

- to provide written consent before the school division may proceed in:
  (a) Pre-placement evaluations
  (b) Your child's initial placement in a program providing special education and related services

- not to be bound by what the school division can offer in services that are needed, but the right to focus in all transactions on what your child needs.

- to a fully paid private school special education placement if your school division refers you to such a setting because it is deemed **appropriate** while the one the school can offer is deemed **not appropriate**.

- to contact the Complaints Officer at your state's Department of Education if you feel the school division has not or is not complying with special education law and regulation. (*See* Appendix C.)

In addition to the rights afforded by P.L. 94–142, which have been detailed on the last several pages, other federal statutes provide additional protection. These laws are highlighted on the two pages which follow.

Selected, Key Federal Statutes Affecting the Education And Civil Rights of Children and Youth with Disabilities*

P.L. 89-10, the Elementary and Secondary Education Act of 1965.

Provided a comprehensive plan for readdressing the inequality of educational opportunity for economically underprivileged children. It became the statutory basis upon which early special education legislation was drafted.

P.L. 89-313, the Elementary and Secondary Education Act Amendments of 1965.

Authorized grants to state institutions and state-operated schools devoted to the education of children with disabilities. It was the first federal grant program specifically targeted for children and youth with disabilities.

P.L. 89-750, The Elementary and Secondary Education Amendments of 1966.

This law amended Title VI of P.L. 89-10 and established the first federal grant program for the education of children and youth with disabilities at the local school level, rather than at state-operated schools or institutions. It established the Bureau of Education of the Handicapped (BEH) and the National Advisory Council (now called the National Council on Disability).

P.L. 91-230, The Education of the Handicapped Act of 1970.

This law amended Title VI of P.L. 89-750 and established a core grant program for local educational agencies. This program is known as Part B. This law also authorized a number of discretionary programs.

P.L. 93-112, The Rehabilitation Act of 1973.

This law provides a comprehensive plan for providing rehabilitation services to all individuals, irregardless of the severity of their disability. It also provided for civil rights enforcement under Section 504. This law was amended by P.L. 98-221 in 1983, and by P.L. 99-506 in 1986.

P.L. 93-380, The Education Amendments of 1974.

These amendments to the Elementary and Secondary Education Act contained two important laws. One is the Education of the Handicapped Act Amendments of 1974. This law was the first to mention the provision of an appropriate education for all children with disabilities. It also reauthorized the discretionary programs. The second important law, the Family Education Rights and Privacy Act, often called the Buckley Amendment, gives parents and students under the age of 18, and students age 18 and over, the right to examine records kept in the student's personal file.

P.L. 94-142, The Education for All Handicapped Children Act of 1975.

This law mandates a free appropriate public education for all children with disabilities, ensures due process rights, mandates education in the least restrictive environment, and mandates Individualized Education Programs, among other things. It is the core of federal funding for special education.

P.L. 98-199, The Education of the Handicapped Act Amendments of 1983.

This law reauthorized the discretionary programs, including the establishment of services to facilitate the transition from school to work for youths with disabilities through research and demonstration projects; the establishment of parent training and information centers; and funding for demonstration projects and research in early intervention and early childhood special education.

P.L. 98-524, The Carl D. Perkins Vocational Education Act of 1984.

This law authorized funds to support vocational education programs to include youths with disabilities. The law stated that individuals who are members of special populations must be provided with equal access to recruitment, enrollment, and placement activities in vocational education.

Reprinted from *News Digest*, Vol. 1, #1, 1991, National Information Center for Children and Youth with Disabilities, Washington, DC

Selected, Key Federal Statutes Affecting the Education And Civil Rights of Children and Youth with Disabilities*

P.L. 99-372, The Handicapped Children's Protection Act of 1986.

This law provides for reasonable attorneys' fees and costs to parents and guardians who prevail in administrative hearings or court when there is a dispute with a school system concerning their child's right to a free appropriate special education and related services.

P.L. 99-457, The Education of the Handicapped Act Amendments of 1986.

This law mandates services for preschoolers with disabilities and established the Part H program to assist states in the development of a comprehensive, multidisciplinary, and statewide system of early intervention services for infants and toddlers (birth to age 3). This law also reauthorized the discretionary programs and expanded transition programs.

P.L. 100-407, The Technology-Related Assistance for Individuals with Disabilities Act of 1988.

The primary purpose of this law is to assist states in developing comprehensive, consumer-responsive programs of technology-related assistance and to extend the availability of technology to individuals with disabilities and their families. Assistive technology device is broadly defined in the law to give the states flexibility in the programs to be developed. Assistive technology services under this law include 8 activities related to developing consumer-responsive services with federal funds.

P.L. 101-127, The Children with Disabilities Temporary Care Reauthorization Act of 1989.

This law is actually a part of a larger federal law, the Children's Justice Act, P.L. 99-401. Title II of this law includes provisions to fund temporary child care (e.g., respite care) for children who have a disability or chronic illness and crisis nurseries for children at risk of abuse or neglect. In 1989, P.L. 101-127 extended and expanded this program for two years and included an increase in funding for these programs from $5 million to $20 million in 1990 and 1991. By July, 1990, 87 grants were awarded to states to develop and establish respite care programs and crisis nurseries.

P.L. 101-336, The Americans with Disabilities Act of 1990.

This law, based on the concepts of the Rehabilitation Act of 1973, guarantees equal opportunity for individuals with disabilities in employment, public accommodation, transportation, State and local government services, and telecommunications. The ADA is the most significant federal law assuring the full civil rights of all individuals with disabilities.

P.L. 101-392, The Carl D. Perkins Vocational and Applied Technology Education Act of 1990.

This law amended P.L. 98-524 for the purpose of making the United States more competitive in the world economy. This law is closely interwoven with the Education of the Handicapped Act (P.L. 94-142) toward guaranteeing full vocational education opportunity for youth with disabilities.

P.L. 101-476, The Education of the Handicapped Act Amendments of 1990.

This law changed the name of EHA to the Individuals with Disabilities Education Act (IDEA). This law reauthorized and expanded the discretionary programs, mandated transition services and assistive technology services to be included in a child's or youth's IEP, and added autism and traumatic brain injury to the list of categories of children and youth eligible for special education and related services.

P.L. 101-496, The Developmental Disabilities Assistance and Bill of Rights Act of 1990.

This law authorizes grants to support the planning, coordination, and delivery of specialized services to persons with developmental disabilities. In addition, this law provides funding for the operation of state protection and advocacy systems for persons with developmental disabilities. The original law was enacted in 1963 by P.L. 88-164. In 1987, P.L. 100-146 significantly expanded the Act to include persons with mental retardation, autism, cerebral palsy, and epilepsy.

* Adapted from: DeStefano and Snauwaert (1989).

Appendix F

Steps Toward the Due Process Procedure

After all discussion with your child's school personnel fails:

Determine the nature of your problem:

If general violation of P.L. 94-142 requirement, file **Complaint** with the State Education Agency; otherwise:

Define the issue.

Contact parent or advocacy group:

Ask for information.

Solicit support.

Utilize private sector professionals.

Request **Mediation**, if desired.

Write **Due Process Appeal** request.

Prepare for **Due Process Hearing**.

Participate in **Due Process Hearing**.

Appeal by requesting **Review** by Department of Education.

Appeal a negative final decision by initiating **Civil Action** in the courts.

Appendix G

College and Post-Secondary Resources

NOTE: Listings are included for information purposes only. No endorsement by the Learning Disabilities Council is intended or implied.

College Entrance Testing Accommodations

- ACT Special Testing   319/337-1332
  ACT Test Administration
  P.O. Box 168
  Iowa City, IA 52243

- SAT Special Testing   609/734-1280
  ETS Test Administration
  Att: Diane Redsinski
  Rosebell Road
  Princeton, NJ 08541

Directories

- *Lovejoy's College Guide for the Learning Disabled.* 1985. Simon & Schuster, Inc., New York, New York.

- *Petersen's Guide to College with Programs for Learning Disabled Students.* 1990. Peterson's Guides. Princeton, New Jersey.

- *Schoolsearch: Guide to Colleges with Programs or Services for Students with Learning Disabilities.* 1990.

(Contact the special education and/or higher education departments of your state's Department of Education (*see* Appendix C) for information on services available through community colleges in your state.)

Other Resources

- *College and the High School Student with Learning Disabilities* by Wrenn, C., Adelman, P., Pike, M. & Wilson, J. Available from Project Learning Strategies, SAC 200, DePaul University, 2323 N. Seminary, Chicago, IL 60614; 312/362-6897

- *College Students with Learning Disabilities* by Wrenn, C. & Segal, L. Available from Project Learning Strategies (address above).

- HEATH Resource Center   800/544-3284

- National Center on Postsecondary Transition for Students with Learning Disabilities. University of CT, Storrs, CT   203/486-4036

- *Unlocking Potential: College and Other Choices for Learning Disabled People: A Step by Step Guide* by Scheiber, B. & Talpens, J. 1987. Adler & Adler, Bethesda, Maryland.

(*See* Appendix B for additional listings.)

Transitional Post-Secondary Programs

- Beacon College   904/787-7660
  105 East Main Street
  Leesburg, FL 34748

- Career Apprenticeship Program   508/888-0489
  Riverview School
  551 Route 6A
  East Sandwich, MA 02537

- Chapel Haven   203/397-1714
  1040 Whalley Avenue
  New Haven, CT 06515-1743

- Landmark College   508/927-4440
  412 Hale Street
  Prides Crossings, MA 01965

- Life Development Institute   602/254-0822
  1720 East Monte Vista
  Phoenix, AZ 85006

- Monmouth Association for Children   201/774-4737
  & Adults with Learning Disabilities
  Apartment Residences
  1501 Park Avenue, Apt. #1
  Asbury Park, NJ 07712

- New York University Para-Educator   212/998-5800
  Center for Young Adults
  One Washington Place
  New York, NY 10003

● Oakdale Foundation, Inc.   413/528-2346
  42 Oak Street
  Great Barrington, MA 01230

● PACE (Professional Assistant   708/570-7200
    Center for Education)
  National College of Education
  2840 Sheridan Road
  Evanston, IL 60201

● Threshold   617/491-3739
  Lesley College
  29 Everett Street
  Cambridge, MA 02138-2790

● VISTA (Vocational, Independence,   203/399-8080
    Supported, Traditional, Alternative)
  1356 Old Clinton Road
  Westbrook, CT 06498

● Woodbridge   412/366-9150
  Pathways Network
  9400 McKnight Road, Suite 106
  Pittsburgh, PA 15237

Case Studies

The following pages include several case studies describing actual people with learning disabilities and their own personal experiences.

As described in Chapter 1, "Learning Disabilities, the Hidden Handicap," individuals with learning disabilities may be found in all walks of life. As was also noted, learning disabilities vary greatly as to the nature and severity of the disability.

Read individually, no one case study is necessarily representative of what learning disabilities are. Read as a group, however, these case studies do provide a glimpse of the diversity of learning disabilities, the manner in which they manifest themselves, and the range of experiences, both positive and negative, which these particular LD individuals have undergone.

The case studies may also serve as a point of discussion for you and your older learning disabled youngster. Many parents have reported that it is helpful to read an article which describes a real learning disabled individual to their own child.

The House Across the Street

by Allen Beyler

Life for me has always been somewhat of a surprise. I feel as though I was born a failure but grew up to be a success.

I came along as the youngest child of three children in a scholastically able family. In my neighborhood in the preschool days I seemed at least as normal as the other kids. Secretly, I felt better than normal in the kinds of pre-school competition. I was quick, hard to catch, hard to find and full of ideas.

My experience in the first and second grades with reading and spelling problems changed most of my ideas about who I am. My parents, my friends, and my teachers were first surprised by the difficulties, then later, troubled by them. I was soon behind and out of the competition, a nice kid but a failure! At this time in school, the middle thirties, there were only three kinds of students, average, bright and stupid. If you weren't average or bright, you had to be stupid. I believed it, others believed it and I soon got a second problem, a pervasive sense of inferiority. It is so easy to become what the system and others around you think you are.

Discovering Creativity

I had some things going for me. My father, a school administrator, had lost hope in me, but my mother hadn't. Mother had taught English and from the very start of my trouble, she committed herself to fixing my problem. She spent hours from first grade on into college, teaching, reading, spelling and correcting work for me. I now see that she didn't improve my reading and spelling very much but what she did for me was help me regain a sense of self-worth. She loved me as I am and she acted it out over and over and over. She also helped me discover my gift of creativity. With her encouragement, I discovered the joy of making things and that I am good at it; better than most. It was this love, this creative success, which made it possible to face school with all the feelings of failure and inferiority.

Carpenters Helped Me to Grow

Another thing I had going for me was the house that was started across the street from ours. It helped to change my life. I was ten and for some reason the carpenters liked me. More than that they let me join in the work right up on the scaffold with them sawing and nailing. They too acted out for me that I was a neat kid. They encouraged me to develop my head and hands skills. When school was helping me to fail, they were helping me to grow.

We are a family of college people, so, at mother's insistence, and with her help, I started college. By this time, I had discovered that science and chemistry were subjects at which I am better than most. I moved in that direction. I also began to learn how to self-advocate. This consisted of talking with teachers about my strengths and weaknesses and making the best deal to work on the course material to get the most from the class. After college and the Korean War, I went back to the University for two years. I studied architecture and discovered more ability and gifts. I now know I have three-dimensional skills which are helpful to artists, builders and others.

Building has been a good solution to my problem. There is no great need to read or write and lots of use for head and hands skills. It answers my need to make things and I use my three-dimensional ability in planning and figuring material. There are many chances for the artist in me to live. People like what I do and tell me so. I am considered a success which is what I have wanted to be from the first grade on.

Editor's Note: *Allen Beyler has been in business as a builder-contractor in Illinois for thirty years. He received a B.S. degree and also studied architecture for two years. He speaks regularly to teachers' groups as part of their inservice training as well as to parents and learning disabled children.*

Reprinted from *Their World* magazine with permission. *Their World* is the annual publication of the National Center for Learning Disabilities, 99 Park Ave., New York, NY 10016. Founder, Carrie Rozelle; President, Anne Ford. *Their World*, 1988, p. 8.

Must There Continue to be Cases Like Jimmy?

My Jimmy is a handsome boy—blond, fair skinned—and his face is dominated by large, brown eyes which are framed with thick, curling lashes. When he smiles, his dark eyes sparkle and there is an aura of sweetness about him. Or at least there used to be— when he was five years old and entering Kindergarten with enthusiasm and eagerness. Now, at age 16, those beautiful eyes are still dark and large, but they do not have that old sparkle. They are dulled from feelings of hostility and fear, which are waiting to be manifested again and again in his behavior. The tragedy of this situation is not peculiar to my son; there are millions more children like him. He is suffering from a language disorder, more commonly known as a learning disability, and he has spent the past 11 years on a treadmill of misunderstanding. He ran hard on that treadmill, but he made no progress forward because today's accelerated education did not provide him with the time, nor the proper teaching techniques, to allow him to master the basic skills of reading, writing, and arithmetic. So my intelligent, sensitive and handsome son might never know the satisfaction of even partial development of his capabilities—but he does know, already, the degrading emotions of fear, insecurity, and bitterness.

Let me tell you of his life as he lived it from 9 a.m. until 3 p.m., five days a week, nine months a year, for 11 years.

Kindergarten was fun at first. He was obviously bright, alert, and active. The teacher liked him because he was attractive, well mannered, and happy. Then one day I noted a rash on the palms of his hands. The doctor said the rash was caused by tension and he prescribed phenobarbital. The rash went away and I forgot about it. His first grade teacher was a loving and skillful person who liked Jimmy tremendously. Then one day she telephoned to suggest that I help Jimmy with his reading. "I feel so sorry for him when he must read aloud. I want so to help him, especially when I see him blinking away the tears." So of course I began to help, but it was soon apparent that flash cards and practice reading at home were not doing the job. Jimmy began to cry frequently. His small voice was hardly audible as he fought through his emotions and tears to tell me how the children in his classroom laughed when he tried to read aloud. "The harder I try, the more they laugh," he said. And so he began working with an educational

therapist twice a week in the early hours before school, so his classmates would not know he had to be tutored.

I learned from his therapist that Jimmy was the victim of dyslexia—one of the many types of learning disabilities which affect fully 20 percent of our nation's school population, irrespective of the social or economic level of the family or community. A dyslexic child does not perceive letters, numbers, and sounds as they are actually written or spoken: b's become d's; "was" becomes "saw." Such a child almost always has the added disadvantage of a short attention span. So the complex function of assimilating sounds and figures and processing them into meaningful words to be written or spoken becomes an impossible task. But, said Jimmy's therapist, the condition could be corrected by appropriate teaching procedures. The tutoring would help, she explained, but I could not expect a miracle. The instructional techniques used by a tutor would be effective in the ultimate degree only if they were reinforced by proper remedial and teaching methods in Jimmy's classroom, and, unfortunately, our school district—like many—was not attuned to the problem. And so Jimmy became the typical textbook example of the bright, but frustrated, learning disabled child.

Jimmy worked hard, but it was with ever-increasing heavy heart. The words and numbers used in the classroom were presented differently from the way the tutor introduced them. In class, Jimmy could not respond in the desired manner. His friends on the playground began to call him "Dummy" and "Stupid."

In the second grade the boys began to play games like baseball at recess, and Jimmy found that he could not catch nor hit the ball so well as his peers. Nor could he decide which hand to use when he tried. He began to dread recess as much as class, and the tears of hurt and embarrassment were more frequent. The teacher said, "Give him time."

By third grade he had no friends, but still he tried desperately to acquire some. I shall never forget the many, many times Jimmy sat beside me as I telephoned mother after mother to invite their children to come to play—and hear the mothers say, "Bobby—or Stevie—doesn't want to play today." How could I tell my child that obviously Bobby—or Stevie—did not want to play with JIMMY? But Jimmy knew. And so Jimmy began a habit pattern of school, home to watch TV or to build a model alone, a tension filled dinner hour with his parents, and then restless sleep. That restlessness increased, and his attention span became even shorter. Also, at school, the disciplinary measures increased in frequency and his teacher's temper became shorter. Again, I discussed the matter with his teacher and was advised to stop the tutoring, so Jimmy could feel that he no longer needed extra help. Unfortunately, I took that advice.

By fifth grade Jimmy could not stay in his seat for more than a few minutes at a time. But he no longer cried nor even told me about school, for he was building his defense mechanisms. He pretended to himself that he did not care about school marks; the school psychologist said Jimmy had developed an emotional block to learning.

So my husband and I took Jimmy to a clinical psychologist for a series of tests. The report told us that Jimmy's perceptual malfunction still existed, but, more importantly, we learned that Jimmy thought of himself as a mental cripple. He was convinced that other children could learn, but he was different: he could not learn. His self-image was extremely poor and his self-confidence was almost non-existent. Something had to be done immediately. But What? Jimmy spent most of his waking hours in the school room, which was where the psychological damage was being done. The school district's special education classes were designed for the retarded, and Jimmy had an excellent I.Q. In addition, placement in such a stigmatizing situation would do further damage to his emotional health. None of the surrounding private day schools employed the special techniques necessary to provide the supportive help that was required, and we did not want to send a 10 year-old boy away to boarding school. So we tried to balance the devastating effects of the failure syndrome by finding an area of endeavor in which he could know some success. We joined a swim club and placed him on the swimming team—where there was no ball to elude him and no report card to embarrass him. God was good to Jimmy. At the end of the swimming season, Jim won the medal for the most improved swimmer. I shall always remember his smile that day: tentative, uncertain, trembling. Did I really win a medal? Am I really worth something after all? Will the other children like me now?

That fall, when Jimmy entered sixth grade, he attended classes in a different school building and he attacked his new environment with a more confident air and his teachers, happily, were warm, caring people who could understand the phrase, "a poor self image." A few weeks after school started, Jimmy brought home

a friend. A friend! By January he had two friends. It was a Glorious year. His grades improved and he actually smiled and laughed when he played. His parents relaxed, even though the symptoms of the disability persisted. Jimmy still misunderstood instructions; he still could not spell; he still was not reading on grade level; he still was not playing baseball, not football. But he could swim well, and he continued to win ribbons and medals. That success balanced the problems in class, so at least he was not deteriorating emotionally. We did not foresee that his seventh grade year would put Jimmy on the road to educational and emotional destruction, by virtue of a teacher's personality. Perhaps you will say that children should learn to adjust to all types of personalities, but can you expect an orchid to bloom on the face of an iceberg? You may say, "Change the teacher." Do you know the rigidity of a large institutional school system? "Then explain to the teacher." We did. Over and over. "Tell the principal." We did. And Jimmy's hands and feet swelled, and the skin broke, and the sores became infected. He was put back on phenobarbital. His self confidence was at a new low and he chose not to continue in the competitive atmosphere of "swimming." His two friends disappeared, but they were replaced by many: boys like Jimmy who had lost all faith in themselves and who distrusted all adults.

By eighth grade, Jimmy and his friends were "cutting" classes frequently. The school counsellor and teachers said Jimmy was both lazy and arrogant. He was termed a troublemaker. "He's never a discipline problem at home," I said, and the school disciplinarian replied, "I wonder why that is."

And so we arranged to send Jim to a good boarding school for his high school years. The day before he was to leave for his new school, his defenses disappeared and he sobbed out his plea to stay in the security of his home. Things would be different in high school, he said. He would work harder; he wouldn't cut class, and he'd find new friends. Jimmy's pediatrician, who had already had long talk sessions with him over the several preceding months, said, "Let him try." And so Jimmy went to school and enrolled.

The high school disciplinarian sought Jim out that very first day and told him he had better behave in that building or be expelled. Jimmy's hope for a new start was destroyed with those few words—but his determination remained. He did try; he did go to class; he did seek out new social relationships. But the hurdle was too high, for class placement, and several teacher personalities, had been chosen without thought for Jimmy's needs. By October he was cutting classes again and we began to suspect that he was resorting to marijuana to block out the reality of his life as he had to live it. We heard again from his teachers that he was obviously bright, but his homework (which he seldom did) was a disgrace. Again we explained that he had dyslexia, but again the word was meaningless to the educators. We wrote to the local school board for help, but their response showed no understanding of the problem.

Jimmy began to vent his hostility by getting into minor scrapes which sometimes necessarily involved the police. (Survey after survey has shown that approximately seventy-five percent of today's juvenile delinquents have a history of learning disabilities.) He never smiled, and his eyes no longer had that sparkle. Resentment and hostility were the only emotions he knew. He failed English and Algebra that year.

Then our, and Jimmy's, hopes were again revived. The school system hired an educational therapist for the high school, and of course we asked that Jimmy be allowed to work with her. Jim was uncooperative at first, but as the therapist earned his trust, he went to her voluntarily—even two and three times in a day. She encouraged him and complimented him at every honest opportunity, and so his wounds began to heal. With great effort he fought to overcome his deficiencies. There was a very high mountain to climb, but at last there was someone at school who understood and who was trying to help. Jim's sweet smile was seen again and he even began to develop a sense of humor. He was so much easier to love!

By the end of the year, I dared to hope that the damage to his ego, in part, had been repaired. He passed every course.

The learning specialist, who helped Jimmy when he was in elementary school, tells me that it is very common reaction for a child like Jimmy to fear success when he is beginning to achieve it. After all, he had lived with failure, fear, and a low self-esteem all his life, and there was so much basic material he did not know. The next class level courses were difficult for him, and he feared that he could not continue to improve. The regular classroom teachers were not knowledgeable in the needs of the disabled adolescent, nor of the classroom techniques that would assist him, so the next year, no one understood that he was still deficient in basic skills and still in need of supportive help and attitudes—for the learning specialist was still working alone, and had time only for the "crisis cases."

At this writing, Jimmy has dropped out of school and he no longer lives at home—self-recrimination makes living at home an intolerable situation for him, for he knows he has disappointed his parents. So he faces the world feeling alone and desperate. His fine mind is being wasted—even a steady job is an unattainable goal because he does not have a high school diploma. He has no faith in himself nor in society. Why should he not rebel? Why should he not wish to punish someone? Sixty percent of the inmates of our nation's prisons are incarcerated in a tangible cage that represents the intangible cage our inadequate educational system built for them, bar by bar, through their school years.

SLD Gazette, November, 1978. Reproduced with the permission of the Massachusetts ACLD.

A Joey Success Story

The names are fictitious: the story is true.

Background: Joey's parents are the "salt of the earth." Father is an office machine repairman. Mother is a tiny 4'8" dynamo who always said, "Joey may not be able to read, but he can do (this) and (this) and (this)." She fought the school bureaucracy for Joey's right to learn. Joey's siblings consist of two older brothers, moderately learning disabled. Joey is the most learning disabled person I have met in over twenty years of teaching.

I met Joey when the town redistricted and he was "dumped" into our third grade for a second time around. How he got to third grade I will never know. He was unable to read the simplest material, and he could do math only on a low first grade level. Needless to say, his classroom teacher was beside herself. She came to me, the reading specialist, to see what could be done.

For seven years prior to my becoming a reading specialist, I had taught a group of children whom "nobody wanted." They had been in grade 1 for a year and had learned little or nothing. Of course they could not go on to grade 2, but the old numbers game was forcing them to go someplace—to me.

I saw to it that Joey spent as much of the day with me as possible. He started the day with my first grade group and stayed for my second and third grade groups. In between, he had short periods alone with me. "Look - Say" was in favor as a reading system, so I taught him phonics, starting with a few letters that could be combined to make words, phrases, and sentences.

To begin, he learned to write from dictation, words then simple sentences. Then he illustrated it. On day 1, he wrote and illustrated. On day 2, he read what he had written the previous day and did another writing and illustration. On day 3, he read the work from days 1 and 2. Then he wrote and illustrated again. On Friday of each week, he could take home a booklet that he had written and could read. By the end of that school year, he had read almost every first grade book in the school and had made considerable progress in math. He was, of course, advanced to grade 4 because one repeat was all that was allowed.

That year our school system instituted one of the first experimental classes of learning disabled students. The eight children with the most serious handicaps in three different schools were gathered together for the morning session and returned to the classroom for the afternoon. Needless to say, Joey was a charter member. He returned to his "home school" for the afternoon sessions where the necessary social studies and science books were taped for him, and the classroom teacher tailored the program so that Joey could participate.

The one class for learning disabled students grew to three classes, and I became the Learning Disabilities Coordinator. The administration only permitted us to have learning disabilities classes for elementary students. I managed to keep Joey with us through seventh grade, but he was getting too old for the class. Something had to be done. No matter what I said or did, there was no way a special program could be instituted for junior or senior high.

I began to search for a private facility, nearby and not too expensive. I found one about twenty miles away and took Joey and his mother to visit near the end of his seventh grade year. He was enrolled. Next began the long, bitter, frustrating, fruitless fight to have the school department pay the tuition. We did manage to get transportation money but no tuition, so Joey's mother became the best Avon lady in the area. At this school, Joey "bloomed." From this school, Joey graduated, one of a class of two.

The time came when Joey wanted a driver's license. He called the Boston Registry, explained that he had a reading disability, and ascertained that if he took his test in Boston, he could bring a "reader" for the exam. If he took the the test in most of the outlying districts, he could not bring a "reader." He would, however, be allowed as much time as he needed to take the exam. Joey went to Plymouth for the test. All other testees had long since left, and the officer said, "You have five minutes to finish." "Oh, no!" said Joey, "Boston told me I could take all day, if necessary, because I have a reading disability." The officer digested this. Then he said, "OK, but if I read it to you, can you finish it up?" "Certainly," said Joey. The officer read. Joey finished and got a passing score. This enabled him to get two part-time custodial jobs with the school department.

Joey was a member of the volunteer fire department, but what he really wanted was to be a member of the ambulance squad. He went to the fire chief who said that he had to take a course which was starting at the high school. He went to an interview with the course instructor and told him of his reading disability. The instructor suggested that he stay for the first session and see what he thought about it. At the end of the session, Joey told the instructor that he thought he could do it. He was given two thick books to read. Joey took them home, a cousin taped them, and each night he sat down with tape recorder and books to read the assigned material. A tape recorder also accompanied him to class.

When exam time came, Joey approached the instructor and reminded him of his reading disability. He was told that it was a three hour exam but that he could do it orally and have four hours in which to do it. Joey was finished with the test in two hours, and when the scores came in, his was the second highest in the class.

Joey took the results of his course efforts to the fire chief and asked for the ambulance job. The fire chief said, "Oh, no, you have to know the names and locations of all the streets in town." Joey went to the Town Hall where he got a street directory and a map. Each night Joey and his father studied the locations of various streets. Then they drove to the streets they had studied by way of several routes. At the end of a month, Joey approached the fire chief again. This time the chief was properly amazed. Joey was made a member of the ambulance crew. No other members of the crew had been required to learn the streets, and they all depend on Joey to get them where they are going.

Now there are frequent telephone calls for Mr. S. coming into Joey's home. His mother used to say, "My husband isn't here now." The caller would say that he (or she) just wanted to thank him for "saving my life in the ambulance last night." "Oh," she would say. "That was my son." To me, she said, "I'm not used to having two Mr. Ss in the house." But Joey is not Joey any longer. He is a man. Joe, Mr. S, has emerged.

Has Joe conquered his reading problem? No. He has, however, learned how to live with it, how to acknowledge it without denigrating himself. Will he ever sit down and read a good book? Probably not, but he can sit down and listen to a good book. He is well acquainted with "Talking Books." Joe may not be able to read, but he can listen to a car and make a fairly accurate diagnosis of its ills. Joe and his father go hunting each fall and always come home with a deer. But no guns for them! They hunt with bows and arrows.

Because of the loving acceptance of Joe, the person, by his family, he has no emotional overlay. Because of careful, intelligent management of his academic life, Joe knows that he is an intelligent being. He is able to admit his handicap, assess a situation, and decide whether it is something that he can or cannot handle. Certainly Joe has a handicap, but so do those with cerebral palsy or hearing and sight problems, or those with crippled limbs. Each person with a handicap must evolve ways to compensate. Joe's way is not to try to hide it (for it truly cannot be hidden long) but to bring it out into the open and work around it. Do fellow workers and friends look down on Joe because of his disability? Not on your life! He does his share of the work, helps others when he can, and accepts help when he needs it. He has self respect and the respect of all who know him.

SLD Gazette, September, 1978. Reproduced with the permission of the Massachusetts ACLD.

Learning–
A Struggle and Challenge

by Karen Campbell

It was the night of the "Celebration of Creativity," the annual fund-raising dinner dance sponsored by the Foundation for Children With Learning Disabilities. I had finished my job of selling raffle tickets and was browsing at the art display the children had done. As I looked at their work, I became rather hypnotized by the crowd noise, and my thoughts started drifting to my remembrances of my childhood.

Memories of my early childhood are filled with frustration, pain and occasions of constant failure. I always knew I was different from the other kids and I was reminded of it every day. I couldn't remember which hand to raise to salute the flag even though instructions had just been given me. In every attempt at writing something, my letters came out backward and I can remember that heat of tears as I struggled to do the simplest task, and failed all too often.

It was like dancing, when you have trouble with the steps or the beat, and you feel awkward. Imagine being surrounded by good dancers and the steps seem so easy, they say "Oh, it's so easy, it's just like this." Time after time you try, but you just can't seem to learn how to dance. So you try to copy other people, or you quit!

My Mind Would Dance Away

I was really quite verbal so I learned how to get by in classroom discussions, but when it came time to read, my mind would dance away and I couldn't remember what I had just read. I couldn't spell the simplest words. I learned how to write poorly, and to clown around or get defensive about my writing and my trouble carrying out instructions.

I never knew it at the time, of course, but I later discovered that the reason for all the trouble I had in school was due to a learning disability—a condition that had nothing to do with intelligence, attitude or personality, but was simply a matter of birth. Like children born color-blind, or suffering a more serious physical flaw, I had come into the world with a disability that would make learning a struggle, and a tremendous challenge.

Not everyone recognized it as such. In school, it had always been the same story: "Karen's such a bright, attractive girl. Her mind just seems to wander. She doesn't pay attention, nor does she seem to want to try."

My mother knew from an early age that I would avoid confrontation, and that I would clown around about my problems. What she didn't know was that I was trying my best, because I wanted so badly to please my parents, but I just couldn't keep up.

I used to hide during recess because the other kids used to tease me.

Despite my problem, I was able to get through elementary, junior high and high school with minimal difficulty because I knew how to drop classes, copy papers, get into study groups with better students, and cheat. I never felt good about any of that, but I knew I had to go to college to please my parents, and it was the only way I knew to get through.

The irony is that my mother always helped me type my reports and rewrote my work for me, and I also have to admit that school in the late 60's and early 70's was none too demanding.

High school was over and I was on my way to college. I knew I wanted to major in speech therapy, because I had a sister who was deaf and needed help with her speech and a mother who had been a speech therapist.

College Was Light Years Over My Head

My first two years in a California Junior College were probably the best years of my life. I had become involved with a man I truly loved and my closest friends were on hand ready to help me through all my classes.

By my junior year, I knew everything was light years over my head. No matter how hard I tried to concentrate, I kept losing track. I had a terrible time keeping up in class. I was constantly trying to copy other people's notes and I was becoming more and more depressed because I couldn't read my own writing.

When it came time to study, I made a habit of getting into two or three study groups and listening the best I could. I copied three sets of notes and I taped all my lectures. Old exams always helped a little, but the most helpful factor was that nearly every class only required a multiple choice examination, and I knew I always could get through a multiple choice test.

By the time graduation and graduate school came up, I managed to improve my writing skills to some degree through the help of an English teacher who became my mentor. She always gave me unconditional support and for the first time in my life, I started to feel good about myself.

I Had Self-Doubt

At the same time, I started to have some self-doubt about my reason for going into Special Education, suspecting that I was just doing it to please my parents. I also began to resent school. I wanted to take some time off, but I knew I couldn't find employment. I had tried several waitress jobs, but on each of them I had a terrible time adding up the checks, or writing checks the chefs could understand.

The one job that put me through school was teaching swimming, but since it wouldn't be available through the fall and because I wanted to get away, I enrolled in a foreign exchange program to teach in Mexico.

I wanted to work in a speech therapy camp, where I could obtain some experience working with a variety of patients. It was to be my first real experience as a therapist and I hoped it would help me reach some decisions about the direction I was heading.

However, I never felt so inadequate in my life. I had no idea what I was supposed to be doing. I couldn't write reports and I had such a great feeling of failing as a therapist that I didn't know what to do when I finally got my first client. I was sure that even this retarded child would find out how incompetent I was and if anyone questioned my ability, I eliminated all doubt by confessing that I couldn't handle the situation. Of course I failed to get the glowing recommendation I needed. The trainers instead suggested that I

look for other means of employment.

I decided the only move left me was to go back to school and try again. I had scheduled my classes so that I would avoid clinic that year, even though I suspected the omission would come back to haunt me.

In the fall, I spent time in the hospital, recovering from surgery to remove a tumor and addiction to pain killers. But a few weeks later I was discharged, I made up my mind that I was going to run in a half-marathon known as the Bidwell Classic.

I Ran the Race

I enjoyed training for the competition and was looking forward to the race when I got a call from my friend, Sandy. Sandy was one of my closer friends who has always been there for me, to help me study and give me support. She also had a way of calming me down.

I thought she had called just to wish me good luck, but I was stunned to find out she was in the hospital recovering from a mastectomy. She had cancer and it was spreading. She told me she wanted me to run the race for her, and that she wanted to see me when I had finished. I later tried to give Sandy my ribbon, but she insisted that I keep it.

That Fall and Spring both of us were sick, Sandy's malignancy continued to grow and I was in and out of the school medical center with Irritable Colon Syndrome—a catch-all diagnosis for psychosomatic ills.

The pressure to stay in school got increasingly difficult. I barely got through each day, and the stress of it all had exacerbated my stomach pain and my addiction to pain killers. I had to drop a few classes, but I got through the semester.

At Christmas I didn't want to go home, partly because I didn't want to hear parents tell me that the cause of my trouble was that I wasn't trying hard enough.

I stopped by to see Sandy, fearing it would be her last Christmas. The cancer had spread to her lungs and neither of us could talk about it. She died a few days into the New Year and I felt it was a great loss.

Nothing to Lose Anymore

I was determined to pass my comprehensive examination and as strange as it may sound I really began to enjoy the challenge. I had finally come to the conclusion, that the biggest fear I had was the fear of failing and that everyone, myself included, was expecting me to fail. With that in mind, I pushed forward because I knew I had nothing to lose anymore.

Passing those comprehensive exams, after running again in the Bidwell Classic, offered up a few obstacles. The department was none too keen about giving me a teaching credential since the feeling was that my writing skills were not up to standard.

After recognizing that I couldn't write, several people in the education department were somewhat embarrassed by me, since I had gone all the way through their system only to fail their writing standards. So I worked even harder after the professors demanded that I be supervised by a third party therapist, and it all worked out to an "A" for me in student teaching.

One battle remained. I had to get myself ready for the Bidwell run and for the comprehensives. My training had suffered while I concentrated my energies on study, but the morning of the race, I virtually hypnotized myself into competitive fitness, and I managed to run the 13-mile course without feeling the stab of pain. I just kept visualizing myself at the end of the finish line happily picking up my T-shirt that I planned to wear into my exams the following week. When the tests did occur, I went into them with a strange sense of calmness. Most of the other graduate students were nervous wrecks, but I was no longer concerned about failure, I just wanted to complete the process. The examinations required that I write for four days straight.

I passed, with test scores that were higher than some of my fellow students.

The Rewards of Struggle

I began to feel the rewards of my long struggle soon after I began working with children. Like me, they also had learning disabilities and were so vulnerable in so many areas. I recognized my problems in them and realized that my physical problem stemmed from the years of holding back the pain I felt.

I have since acquired understanding about my learning disabilities, but more important, I have learned there isn't anything I can't do if I really want it badly enough.

I've also come to know some people with learning disabilities who say they are glad they had to maintain their struggle.

I know that mine has made me a better person for it all.

Reprinted from *Their World* magazine with permission. *Their World* is the annual publication of the National Center for Learning Disabilities, 99 Park Avenue, New York, NY 10016. Founder, Carrie Rozelle; President, Anne Ford. *Their World*, 1988, pp.42–43

Randy Brookshire has unusual distinction of being on two winning teams at Virginia

The Winner
Cavs' Brookshire overcomes demands, long odds

By Bob Lipper
Times-Dispatch staff writer

Charlottesville - Randy Brookshire, an offensive tackle for The University of Virginia's football team, was talking recently with a fellow student about their Social Analysis 402 class. There was some discussion of a paper Brookshire was writing on the nuclear arms race and some griping about the midterm test the professor had just given. The grades were to be posted that afternoon.

"I'm not gonna go pick up the test," said Brookshire. "I don't want to go to practice with a bad attitude."

He grinned. Still, if you know anything about Brookshire's case, the implication was plain: Juggling the demands of football and academics hasn't come easy for Brookshire, whose playing days in Scott Stadium end with Saturday's game against Virginia Tech. As a football player, he's battled back from injuries, a position switch and a mid-career demotion from first-string status. And as a student, he's overcome obstacles few others at the university face.

Having a good attitude helps...

Brookshire knew he wasn't stupid. He thought he might be a tad lazy, but even that didn't fully explain to him the difficulties he was having as a high school student in Poquoson, a riverside community that borders Hampton. He was articulate. And he had a quick mind. But when it came to translating a teacher's words to note paper or to comprehending a paragraph in his history textbook or to memorizing a table of chemical substances without getting confused or to handling an English quiz without coming unglued, he had trouble.

He was learning disabled. He didn't know it at the time. All he knew was that the C's and B's that dominated his report cards seemed to come with great difficulty. Other than that, he kept his wits about him and got by. "What I couldn't do," he says, "I would fake. And what I couldn't fake, I wouldn't do." Besides, he was good at sports. Among some faculty members, that counted for something.

So he drifted through school. And when things went awry – when he was confronted by situations he wasn't equipped to handle – his frustration erupted into antisocial outbursts. It was a defense mechanism.

"Sometimes I'd get cornered," he recalls. "Instead of doing it, I'd just cause trouble. If you read anything about the learning disabled, I was a classic case. LD kids are hyperactive, they're trouble makers. I was always impatient, always getting tossed out of class. Those are classic signs. If you're standing outside the classroom, you can't get asked questions."

Several teachers suspected something was wrong, that Brookshire's problems were more deep-seated than mere thick-headedness or perversity. But no steps were taken. Remember: This was 6-8 years ago, and evaluation and special programs for the learning disabled were not as routine nor as sophisticated as they are today. Brookshire's saving grace was that he's very bright. "If he wasn't so intelligent," says Poquoson principal Ray Vorhauer, "he might've just been cast off as a dummy."

Brookshire was lucky. Mostly he was lucky to have Vorhauer for a principal and Mary Beth Levitt for a chemistry teacher. Brookshire was in the 11th grade when he took Levitt's course. One of Levitt's requirements was that her students memorize a chart of chemical reactions. Brookshire couldn't do it. Try as he might, he flat couldn't do it. Levitt thought at first he wasn't applying himself. Then she began to wonder....

"She thought it was strange that I could talk well in class and that I was brighter than most of the kids," says Brookshire, "but that on tests I'd get blown away."

Levitt and Vorhauer conferred. They suspected a learning disability, and they approached Alva and Patricia Brookshire to see if they'd allow their son to be tested. This was a touchy issue. To have their child labeled as LD or placed in special education classes is something that repels some parents. They don't want their children stigmatized as being different or slow or—the worst—retarded.

The Brookshires, both of whom are civilian employees at Hampton Roads military bases, became convinced that the tests could make a difference for Randy. And so – at the tail-end of his junior year – he took them. The results came back early the following school year. And they revealed that Brookshire had three or four severe learning disabilities – as well as an IQ in the 140's.

"Like my mind doesn't deal with phonics," he says. "I can't sound words out. The only reason I know how to spell 'class,' say, is that I've seen the word before. That's how I spell. People don't realize they spell a lot of words by sounding them out. I can't do that."

The basic skills of reading and writing, so elementary to a standard education, also are elusive for him, "It's such a chore for me to read," he says. "When most people read, they read a sentence and pick the meaning up. The way I read, I read each word and miss the meaning. It's just hard for my mind to hold the words I read. As far as writing, it takes me forever to do a paper. I gave up taking notes after the first year (at Virginia). A lot of people can listen and write the words down at the same time. I can't. I have to think about what I'm writing down, and by that time I've missed half of what's being said. I used to tape record stuff, but with football, I didn't have the time to screen the tapes."

He shrugs. He's 6-3 and weighs about 270 pounds, and he was given his nickname, Buddha, early on at U. Va. for a belly that one might describe as still ample. "It's not just like dyslexia, where I see things upside down and backwards," he says. "For instance, I understand what you're saying, but I can't put it down on paper. Trying to take notes for me in class is useless. That's why I'm in sociology. Sociology deals with large ideas. I have trouble with details, but I can remember the theory."

In any event, the discovery that he was learning disabled partly freed and partly angered Brookshire. Freed him because it gave him new insight into his difficulties and led to the provision of services and programs to help remedy the problems. Angered him because he wondered: why me?

"I feel I'm a pretty intense person," he says. "I've always felt I give more effort at things than the average person. So it really bothered me I wasn't getting A's in school. When my senior year rolled around (and the test results were in), I knew it wasn't my fault, but I still felt I was getting shortchanged. Even now, I still get ticked off every now and then."

At Poquoson, he channeled much of his energy into football. He made all-region and was chased by recruiters. When they found out he was learning disabled, their responses were mixed. "A number of them just said, 'Don't worry about it, we'll get you through,' " says Vorhauer. Only Virginia and Richmond said they'd provide a support system that specifically would deal wih Brookshire's needs, and Richmond would have to utilize services being offered at Virginia Commonwealth. That was one major reason Brookshire chose Virginia—but not the only one. "I just knew I'd go away and flunk out," he says, smiling, "so I thought, if I'm gonna flunk out of school, I want to go to a hard school."

Academically prestigious, Virginia certainly is hard, even for a hand-picked athlete who gets more guidance and tutoring help than most students. Frankly, then-coach Dick Bestwick wondered if Brookshire could survive. "Just before he offered the scholarship," says Vorhauer, "Bestwick called me. He asked me, 'Are you sure he can do the extra work it will take him to get through here?' I said, 'There's no question in my mind.' "

Since then, Brookshire has justified the faith others invested in him. Now in his fifth year at U. Va., he's fought through semesters and summer sessions to register a 2.2 grade average on a 4.0 scale. He's on target to graduate next May unless he detours for a shot at the United States Football League. But he will get his degree. Of that, he is dead certain.

"My parents have been so supportive of me," he says. "They're gonna be so proud when I get my degree. And, yeah, I'm gonna be real proud of myself."

Others will be cheering in the background. His rooting section at Poquoson High will be among them. "Randy really changed the perception of people here about what LD kids were like," says Vorhauer. "And he's changed the self-image of some LD kids. We've had some real success stories here, and Randy was a starting point."

Now the end is in sight for him. School still isn't easy ("The work never lets up, and once you get behind it's a hassle to catch up"), but he keeps plugging. He figures the effort will be worth it one day.

"I've had to do so many things that are so difficult," he says, "I feel I'll be like a shark in a fishbowl when I get into the business world."

And football? That, too, has been a story of perseverance. He lost the 1980 season to an injury. He started at guard in 1981 and for the first four games of 1982 before being switched to tackle and demoted to the second team. He was discouraged. Yet, he kept pushing, improved significantly last spring and emerged as the starter at right tackle. He's the spiritual leader of the offensive line. He's also had a heck of a senior year.

Brookshire has another distinction. Counting the 6-5 finish of 1979, he's shared in two of the Cavaliers three winning records of the last 31 years. "The always-losing attitude bothered me when I first got here," he says. "I didn't lose much in high school. I felt I was gonna be a winner for the years I was here."

He has been.
In more ways than one.

Reprinted with permission from the *Richmond Times-Dispatch*, November 16, 1983.

Additional Reading

Appendices B and C of this guide list resources and organizations which provide information on learning disabilities; contact each organization directly.

In addition, the following pages from the Learning Disabilities Association of America (LDAA) include the titles of numerous publications covering a wide range of topics. These may be purchased and ordered directly from LDAA, as noted on the last page of their form.

Learning Disabilities Association of America

4156 Library Road - Pittsburgh, PA 15234

1/91

QUANTITY	AUTHOR	PUBLICATION	PRICE EACH	TOTAL

ADOLESCENT - YOUNG ADULT

QUANTITY	AUTHOR	PUBLICATION	PRICE EACH	TOTAL
_____	ACLD	Guide Lines for Learning Disabled College Students	1.00	_____
_____	ACLD	L.D. Adult Programs/Services/Independent Living	1.25	_____
_____	ACLD, Inc.	Specific Learning Disabilities in the Adult Years	1.00	_____
_____	ALLEY/DESHLER	Teaching the Learning Disabled Adolescent: Strategies and Methods	37.00	_____
_____	BARBARO, FRED	A Shopper's Guide to Colleges Serving the Learning Disabled College Students	3.00	_____
_____	BROWN, D.	Steps to Independence for People with LD	2.00	_____
_____	CHESLER, BARBARA M.	A Talking Mouth Speaks About Learning Disabled College Students	3.50	_____
_____	CRUICKSHANK, W.	Adolescence & L.D. (A Time Between)	1.00	_____
_____	GAJAR, ANNA H.	Programming for College Students with Learning Disabilities	28.00	_____
_____	GARNETT, K./LaPORTA, S.	Dispelling the Myths: College Students & Learning Disabilities	4.50	_____
_____	GRIGGS, M.J./WIAR, C.	Living with a Learning Disability - A Handbook for High School and College Students	3.00	_____
_____	GUETZLOE, E.	Suicide & Depression, the Adolescent Epidemic: Educations Responsibility	6.50	_____
_____	HUMAN RESOURCES CENTER VOCATIONS REHAB.	From High School to College: Keys to Success for Students with Learning Disabilities	18.00	_____
_____	IOWA ACLD	Survival Skills for the Student with LD	12.00	_____
_____	KRUGER SMITH, BERT	Inside Out or Outside In? (Perceptions of the Learning Disabled Young Person)	2.00	_____
_____	LIFE SKILLS EDUCATION	Youth & Suicide	2.25	_____
_____	MANGRUM/STRICHART	College and the L.D. Student	37.00	_____
_____	ROBERTS, DENNIS	Job Application Language	4.95	_____
_____	SCHEIBER/TALPERS	Unlocking Potential: College and Other Choices for Learning Disabled People	12.95	_____
_____	SERVICES DIVISION	How to Succeed in College	19.00	_____
_____	SMITH, B.K.	Preparing for Tomorrow Young LD's (O)LD	1.50	_____
_____	VOGEL, S.	The College Student with a Learning Disability	5.50	_____
_____	WREN, ADELMAN, PIKE, WILSON	College and the High School Student with Learning Disabilities Student's Perspective	3.50	_____
_____	WREN/SEGAL	College Students with Learning Disabilities - A Student's Perspective	3.00	_____
_____	NATIONAL EASTER SEAL SOCIETY	YES YOU CAN! A Booklet to Help Young People with LD Understand and Help Themselves	3.00	_____

ADOLESCENT - L.D. DELINQUENCY

QUANTITY	AUTHOR	PUBLICATION	PRICE EACH	TOTAL
_____	BOYSTOWN	Clues of L.D. for the Juvenile Justice System	10/1.50	_____
		50/5.00	100/7.50	_____
_____	BERHMANN, P.	WHY ME?	6.00	_____
_____	CRAWFORD, DOROTHY	The ACLD-R&D Project: A Study Investigating the Link Between L.D. and Juvenile Delinquency	4.00	_____
_____	MINNESOTA ACLD	JD/LD Where Do We Go From Here?	4.50	_____
_____	STUTT, H.	Learning Disabilities and the Young Offender: Arrest to Disposition	10.00	_____

AUDITORY

QUANTITY	AUTHOR	PUBLICATION	PRICE EACH	TOTAL
_____	CASSIE, DHYAN	The Auditory Training Handbook for Good Listeners	8.50	_____
_____	GILLET, PAMELA, Ph.D.	AUDITORY PROCESSES	8.00	_____
_____	GRIDLEY, C. MARK	Children Who Can Hear But Can't Listen	3.00	_____
_____	SALEEBY, NANCY, M.S.	Treating Auditory Processing Disorders	4.25	_____
_____	TANSLEY, A.E.	Perceptual Training, Ages 4-11	12.95	_____

BEHAVIOR MODIFICATION

QUANTITY	AUTHOR	PUBLICATION	PRICE EACH	TOTAL
_____	ANDERSON, C.	Symptoms, Signs & Behavioral Abnormalities	.25	_____
_____	LANGFORD/JOHNSON	Behavior Modification and Beginning Reading	1.00	_____
_____	WACKER, J.	The Dyslogic Syndrome	2.00	_____

CHILDREN'S BOOKS

QUANTITY	AUTHOR	PUBLICATION	PRICE EACH	TOTAL
_____	CONCEPT BOOKS Preschool - Grade 3	My Little Foster Sister	5.00	_____
_____	GEHRET	Learning Disabilities and the Don't-Give-Up-Kid: Helps LD kids to learn more about themselves	9.00	_____
_____	MOSS, D.	Shelley, The Hyperactive Turtle	12.95	_____
_____	MUNSCH	Love You Forever: Little boy stages of childhood and manhood	5.50	_____
_____	SCHNEIDER EDUCATIONAL	Turtle Magic (Finger Puppet Included)	5.95	_____
_____	SCHNEIDER EDUCATIONAL	Bunny Magic (Finger Puppet Included)	5.95	_____

QUANTITY	AUTHOR	PUBLICATION	PRICE EACH	TOTAL
		DIRECTORIES		
_____	ACLD	List of Colleges/Universities That Accept Students with LD	4.00	_____
_____	ACLD	Summer Camp Directory	3.00	_____
_____	ARENA, J.	Directory of Educational Facilities for LD Students	4.00	_____
_____	KRONICK, D.	LD - Guide for Directors of Specialized Camps	3.50	_____
_____	KRONICK, D.	LD - Camp Directors Guide on Integration	3.50	_____
_____	KRONICK, D.	LD - Parents Guide to Camping	4.00	_____
_____	MANGRUM/STRICHART	Peterson's - Colleges with Programs for Learning Disabled Students	22.95	_____
_____	SKYER, R./ SKYER, G.	What Do You Do After High School?	31.95	_____
_____	STRAUGHN, CHARLES T. II	Lovejoy's College Guide for the Learning Disabled (Revised Edition)	12.95	_____
		DYSLEXIA		
_____	MILES/GILROY	DYSLEXIA at College	12.95	_____
_____	DUANE/ROME	The Dyslexic Child	7.00	_____
_____	DUFFY/GESCHWIND	Dyslexia - A Neuroscientific Approach to Clinical Evaluation	40.00	_____
_____	GOLDBERG/SCHIFFMAN	Dyslexia - Interdisciplinary Approaches to Reading Disabilities	33.95	_____
_____	GRIFFITHS, A.	Teaching the Dyslexic Child	6.00	_____
_____	LISTON/CROSBY	Dyslexia, What You Can & Can't Do About It	2.50	_____
_____	MILES, T.R.	Dyslexia - The Pattern of Difficulties	33.50	_____
_____	SAVAGE, J.F.	Dyslexia - Understanding Reading Problems	11.50	_____
_____	SMITH, B.K.	Dilemma of a Dyslexic Man	2.50	_____
		EARLY CHILDHOOD		
_____	CORDONI, B.	To Play Is To Learn	3.00	_____
_____	FREIDUS, E.	The Earliest Years	2.00	_____
_____	SCHNEIDER, M.	A Guide to Communication Development Preschool Children: Birth - Five Years	8.50	_____
		FINE MOTOR		
_____	CASEBEER	Developing Motor Skills for Early Childhood Education	5.00	_____
_____	TANSLEY, A.E.	Motor Education, Ages 4-11	12.95	_____
		HYPERACTIVITY/ATTENTION DEFICIT DISORDER		
_____	BLACK, B.	The Hyperactive Child	.50	_____
_____	BLUETT, T.B., SR.	Conquering Low Impulse Control (Program of Treatment for M.B.D. Syndrome (Hyperkinesis/ADD)	7.95	_____
_____	CENTERWALL, S.A., M.D./ CENTERWALL, W.R., M.D.	HYPERKINESIS (A.D.H.D.)	2.50	_____
_____	CIMA, C.	Coping with the Hyperactive Child	1.00	_____
_____	COLEMAN, W.S., MD	Attention Deficit Disorders and Hyperactivity	7.50	_____
_____	CROOK, W., MD	Can What a Child Eat Make Him Dull, Stupid/Hyperactive?	2.00	_____
_____	CROOK, Wm. G.	Solving the Puzzle of Your Hard-to-Raise Child	17.95	_____
_____	EISENBERG, L.	The Overactive Child (Reprint)	1.00	_____
_____	ENTE, G., Dr.	Guidelines for Living with a Hyperactive Child	.50	_____
_____	FRIEDMAN/DOYAL	Attention Deficit Disorder and Hyperactivity (2nd edition)	12.00	_____
_____	HAFNER, C., RN	Learning to Parent a Hyperactive Child	8.95	_____
_____	JORDON, D.	Attention Deficit Disorder - ADD Syndrom	11.00	_____
_____	KINSBOURNE/SWANSON	Hyperactivity	2.00	_____
_____	LEVINE, MELVIN M.D.	(Reprint) ATTENTION DEFICITS: The Diverse Effects of Weak Control Systems in Childhood	3.00	_____
_____	NICHAMIN, S./WINDEL, J.	A New Look at Attention Deficit Disorder	3.00	_____
_____	RAPP, D., M.D.	Allergies and the Hyperactive Child	9.50	_____
_____	SILVER, L., M.D.	ADHD - Attention Deficit-Hyperactivity Disorder and Learning Disabilities (for Parents)	2.00	_____
_____	SILVER, L., M.D.	ADHD - Attention Deficit-Hyperactivity Disorder and Learning Disabilities (for Teachers)	2.00	_____
_____	SILVER, L., M.D.	(Reprint) Controversial Approaches to Treating Learning Disabilities and Attention Deficit Disorder	3.00	_____
_____	SLOANE/ASSADI/LINN	Attention Deficit Disorder in Teenagers and Young Adults	3.00	_____
_____	SLOANE/ASSADI/LINN	Educational Strategies for Students with ADD	3.00	_____
_____	WALKER, N.K./ADLER, S.J.	Visual - Motor Performance ADT	2.00	_____
_____	WALKER, S. III!	Hyperkinesis & Learning Disorders as Symptoms of Medical Problems	1.00	_____
_____	WENDER, P.H., M.D.	The HYPERACTIVE Child, Adolescent, and Adult	7.95	_____
_____	WILD, C.T.	How to Cure Hyperactivity	11.95	_____
_____	WUNDERLICH, R.	Treatment of the Hyperactive Child	1.25	_____

QUANTITY	AUTHOR	PUBLICATION	PRICE EACH	TOTAL
		LANGUAGE		
_____	BEVERIDGE/WAVERING, A.	Expressive Language Remediation for the Older Elementary Child	11.00	_____
_____	WEISS/WEISS	Basic Language Kit	11.75	_____
_____	WIIG, E., Ph.D.	(Reprint) Strategic Language Use in LD Adolescents: An Educational Concern	1.00	_____
		LEGAL		
_____	BOGIN, M.D./GOODMAN, B.	Representing Learning Disabled Children: A Manual for Attorneys	15.00	_____
_____	ROBERTS	Legal Rights Primer	6.00	_____
		MATH		
_____	GOLICK, M.	Deal Me In (The use of playing cards in Teaching and Learning)	9.50	_____
_____	HOROWITZ, R.	Teaching Mathematics to Students with Learning Disabilities	2.00	_____
_____	TREFF/JACOBS	Basic Mathematics Skills	18.00	_____
_____	TREFF/JACOBS	Basic Mathematics Skills - Teacher's Guide	14.00	_____
		MENTAL HEALTH		
_____	ACLD INC.	Taking the First Step . . . Toward Understanding of Good Mental Health and Learning Disabilities	3.00	_____
_____	MALONEY, R.J.	How to Cure Low Self-Esteem	8.00	_____
_____	NAT'L. MTL. HLTH. ASSOC.	Mental Health is 1 2 3	.50	_____
_____	NAT'L. MTL. HLTH. ASSOC.	Adolescent Depression	.50	_____
_____	NAT'L. MTL. HLTH. ASSOC.	Feeling Good About Yourself: Teens and Self-Esteem	1.00	_____
_____	NAT'L. MTL. HLTH. ASSOC.	The Best Years of Your Life? A Teenager's Guide to Surviving Stress	1.00	_____
_____	STAR, N.	Was I Misdiagnosed? Thoughts for Mental Health Professionals	1.00	_____
_____	STEELE, Wm.	Preventing Teenage Suicide	5.00	_____
		MISCELLANEOUS		
_____	ACLD	ACLD Governmental Affairs: A Guide to Membership Action	2.00	_____
_____	ACLD, INC.	Advocacy Training Programs Levels I, II, III	17.00	_____
_____	ACLD, INC.	Pins	2.00	_____
_____	ANTELL, B.	Clothing & Grooming Manual for Special Young Men	2.00	_____
_____	BOY SCOUTS OF AMERICA	Scouting and the Learning Disabled (A Manual for Scouting Leaders)	5.50	_____
_____	BUSCAGLIA, L.	Leo in San Francisco - Bridges Not Barriers	2.00	_____
_____	HAIRE, D.	How the F.D.A. Determines the "Safety" of Drugs	2.00	_____
_____	KRIPPNER	Illicit Drug Usage: Hazards for Learning Disability Students	1.00	_____
_____	LEARNING, INC.	The Learning Inc. Dictionary of Learning Handicaps	2.00	_____
_____	NEEDLEMAN, H.	Deficits in Psychologic & Classroom Performance of Children with Elevated Dentine Lead Levels	1.25	_____
_____	NEEDLEMAN, H.	Terata Babies Defect Crisis	1.25	_____
_____	SEIFERT, DR. C.D.	Autistic Art (Drawing by Autistic Children to Understand the Syndrome)	2.00	_____
_____	WALLACE, B./COOPER, K.	The Citizen's Guide to Lead - Uncovering a Hidden Health Hazard	11.50	_____
		NEUROSCIENCE		
_____	ACLD	1980 - Encounters Backgrounder, Speakers from Scientific Studies Workshop	3.50	_____
_____	ASSOC. FOR RETARDED CITIZENS	Have You Heard . . . About Alcohol & Pregnancy	3.00	_____
_____	COBURN, L., MSW	Drugs and Alcohol	3.00	_____
_____	GOODMAN, D., Ph.D.	Inside the Alcoholic's Brain	4.00	_____
_____	GOODMAN, D., Ph.D.	Nix the Mix - An exploration of the new research area of study when teenagers mix alcohol and pot	4.00	_____
_____	GOODMAN, D., Ph.D.	10 Starting New Facts About Brain Damage & Marijuana	4.00	_____
_____	LEWIS, M.	L.D. and Prenatal Risk	31.00	_____
_____	MORRISON, D.C.	Neurobehavioral and Perceptual Dysfunction in Learning Disabled Children	26.00	_____
_____	SMITH, SHELLY	Genetics and Learning Disabilities	26.00	_____
		NUTRITION		
_____	COTT, A., M.D.	Dr. Cott's Help for Your Learning Disabled Child. The Orthomolecular Treatment	16.95	_____
_____	CROOK, G.W.	Hypoclycemia (Low Blood Sugar)	2.50	_____
_____	CROOK, G.W.	Yeasts and How They Can Make You Sick	2.50	_____
_____	CROOK, G.W.	Tracking Down Hidden Food Allergies	6.75	_____
_____	CROOK, W., M.D.	You & Alergy	2.00	_____
_____	CROOK, W.G.	The Allergic Tension-Fatigue Syndrome	1.00	_____
_____	HOFFER, A.	Children with Learning & Behavioral Disorders	.50	_____
_____	KERSHNER, J.	Megavitamins & Learning disorder: A Controlled Double Blind Experiment	.50	_____

QUANTITY	AUTHOR	PUBLICATION	PRICE EACH	TOTAL
		NUTRITION (cont.)		
_____	McELGUNN, B.	Food and Substance Effects on Brain and Behavior	.75	_____
_____	PERSON, H.	Physical is Fundamental: An Intro.	2.00	_____
_____	POWERS, H.	Dietary Measures to Improve Behavior & Achievement	1.00	_____
_____	RALSTON PURINA	Step-by-Step Pictorial Cookbook	4.00	_____
_____	WACKER, J.	Eliminating the Additives	1.00	_____
		PARENTS		
_____	ACLD OF CONNECTICUT	Parents Assistance Program - A Bridge between Parents and School Systems Working to Obtain the Right Educational Program for Each Child	3.50	_____
_____	ARENT, R.P.	Stress and Your Child	7.95	_____
_____	BARTZ, W.R., PH.D./ RASOR, R.A., ED.D.	Surviving with Kids	9.00	_____
_____	BECK, J.	Minimal Brain Dysfunction	1.00	_____
_____	BEHRMANN/MILLMAN	Excel 1: Experiences for Children in Living	8.00	_____
_____	BEHRMANN/MILLMAN	Excel 2: Body Image	8.00	_____
_____	BETE, C.	What Every Parent Should Know About L.D.	1.25	_____
_____	BEVER, S.	Building a Child's Self-Image - A Guide for Parents	7.00	_____
_____	BONDI, E.	Bayou Bound	1.75	_____
_____	BRIGGS, D.C.	Your Child's Self-Esteem	9.95	_____
_____	BROWN/CONNELLY	How to Organize Your Child & Save Your Sanity	2.50	_____
_____	CLARK, L.	S.O.S.! Help for Parents	9.95	_____
_____	COBURN, L., MSW	Drug Abuse and Your Child	3.00	_____
_____	COOLSEN, P./SELIGSON, M./ GARBARINO, J.	When School's Out and Nobody's Home	4.50	_____
_____	COORDINATING COUNCIL FOR HANDICAPPED CHILDREN	How to Get Services by Being Assertive	7.00	_____
_____	CUMMINGS/MADDUX	Parenting the Learning Disabled	24.00	_____
_____	D'ANTONI/MINIFIE/MINIFIE	A Parent's Guide to Learning Disabilities-Understanding and Helping Your Child	4.00	_____
_____	DUCHARME, Ph.D.	Successful Parenting: A Guide to Stronger Families for Mothers and Fathers	3.00	_____
_____	DUNCAN, L.	Learning Disabilities: Why Some Smart People Can't Learn	1.00	_____
_____	ELIASON/RICHMAN, Ph.D.	A Guide to Learning Disabilities	5.50	_____
_____	FLOWERS, A.	Helping the Child with a Learning Disability	2.00	_____
_____	GOLDBERG/DiVITTO	Born Too Soon	11.95	_____
_____	GORDON, T.	"I Hear You" - Preventing Child Abuse	2.00	_____
_____	GORDON, T.	What Every Parent Should Know	3.50	_____
_____	GREENE, L.J.	Learning Disabilities and Your Child	9.95	_____
_____	GUARENDI, R.N.	You're a Better Parent Than You Think!	9.50	_____
_____	HARWAY, V.	Psychological Assessment of the L.D. Child: A Guide for Parents	1.00	_____
_____	HAWES/WEISS/WEISS	How to Raise Your Child to be a Winner	11.00	_____
_____	HAYS, M.	The Tuned-In, Turned-On Book About Learning Problems	6.00	_____
_____	KELLY, M.	The Mother's Alamanac II: Your Child from Six to Twelve	12.95	_____
_____	KRONICK, D.	The Family & Learning Disabilities	2.00	_____
_____	LAUGHY, LINWOOD	The Interactive Parent: How to Help Your Child Survive and Succeed in the Public School	12.00	_____
_____	LETHINEN, L.	Have You Ever Known a Perceptually Handicapped Child?	.50	_____
_____	LIFE SKILLS EDUCATION	Self Image	2.50	_____
_____	LIFE SKILLS EDUCATION	Family Stress	2.50	_____
_____	MALONEY, R.J., M.A.	Helping Your Child Learn at School	3.00	_____
_____	McCAFFREY, F./FISH, T.	Profiles of the Other Child: A Sibling Guide for Parents	3.50	_____
_____	MINDE, K.	A Guide for Parents on Hyperactivity in Children	4.50	_____
_____	MULTILINGUAL ELEM. SCHOOL PROGRAM	In Any Language: Parents Are Teachers (English/Spanish)	8.00	_____
_____	N.C.C.E.	Parents Organizing to Improve Schools	4.75	_____
_____	NICHAMIN, S./WINDELL, J.	Coping with Your Inattentive Child: A Practical Guide for Management	3.00	_____
_____	OSMAN, B.	Learning Disabilities: A Family Affair (Paperback)	4.95	_____
_____	OSMAN, B.	No One to Play With (Paperback)	11.00	_____
_____	PACER CENTER	Unlocking Doors - How to work better with my child's school & teachers	3.50	_____
_____	PURCER, E./WINDELL, J.	Building Children's Self-Esteem	3.00	_____
_____	RAPP, D.J./BAMBERG, D.	The Impossible Child: A guide for caring teachers and parents in school/at home	11.50	_____
_____	RIMLAND, I.	The Furies and the Flame	15.00	_____
_____	RIPLEY/CVACH	Reprint: Choosing a Doctor for Your Child with Learning Disabilities or Attention Deficit Disorder	2.00	_____
_____	ROSNER, J.	Helping Children Overcome L.D. (Paperback)	16.95	_____
_____	SAMET, L.	Johnny Can Read (Handbook for Parents)	13.95	_____
_____	SCHIMMEL, D./FISCHER, L.	Parents, Schools and the Law	11.95	_____
_____	SCHOONOVER, R.	Handbook for Parents of Children with L.D.	8.00	_____
_____	SEARCY, S.	Teaching Social Skills to Young Children: A Parent's Guide	18.00	_____

QUANTITY	AUTHOR	PUBLICATION	PRICE EACH	TOTAL

PARENTS (cont.)

QUANTITY	AUTHOR	PUBLICATION	PRICE EACH	TOTAL
_____	SHORE, K.	The Special Education Handbook: "A Guide for Parents & Educators"	15.95	_____
_____	SILVER, L.B.	The Misunderstood Child (Paperback)	8.95	_____
_____	SMITH, B.K.	Feelings Are a Family Affair	.50	_____
_____	WILSON	Parent's Guide to "Teacherese": A Glossary of Special Education Terms	7.00	_____
_____	WINDELL, J./WINDELL, E.	Effective Discipline: A Guide to Child Management for Parents	3.00	_____
_____	SMITH, .S.	No Easy Answers (The L.D. Child) (Paperback)	4.95	_____
_____	SMITH/W.R. CENTERWALL/ S.A. CENTERWALL	An Introduction to Your Child Who Has a Learning Disability	2.50	_____
_____	STEVENS, S.H.	Helping the LD Student with Homework	5.00	_____
_____	STEVENS, S.H.	The Learning Disabled Child: Ways That Parents Can Help	9.00	_____
_____	WAGONSELER/McDOWELL	You and Your Child (A Common Sense Approach to Successful Parenting)	11.25	_____
_____	WOLF, A.	Tutoring Is Caring	19.95	_____
_____	WOOLLACOTT, E.	May We Walk in His Shoes	3.50	_____

PHYSICIANS

QUANTITY	AUTHOR	PUBLICATION	PRICE EACH	TOTAL
_____	BERKOWITZ, M., M.D.	A Primer on School Mental Health	12.95	_____
_____	CLEMENTS, S./PETERS, J.	Minimal Brain Dysfunctions in Children: Concepts and Categories	1.00	_____
_____	CONNOLLY, C.	Physicians Guide to L.D.	4.00	_____
_____	DeQUIROS/SCHRAGER	Neuropsychological Fundaments in Learning Disabilities	15.00	_____
_____	GADDES, W.H.	Learning Disabilities: The Search for Causes	2.00	_____
_____	GOLEMAN, D.	A New Computer Test of the Brain	1.00	_____
_____	KAYE, H.	Neurometric Battery: Biochemical, Neurological	.50	_____
_____	MANN/GREENSPAN	The Identification & Treatment of Adult Brain Dysfunction	1.00	_____
_____	REES/CAMPBELL	Patterns of Trace Minerals in the Hair & Relationship to Clinical States (Reprint)	50	_____
_____	REES, E., M.D.	Aluminum Toxicity as Indicated by Hair Analysis	1.00	_____
_____	S. KARGER AG BASEL	Developmental Pharmacology & Therapeutics (Journal of Developmental Pharmacology & Therapeutics,) (10/87) Selected papers on developmental pharmacology and toxicology, (ACLD International Conference.)	32.00	_____

SOCIAL PERCEPTION

QUANTITY	AUTHOR	PUBLICATION	PRICE EACH	TOTAL
_____	BADER, B.	Social Perception & Learning Disabilities	6.00	_____
_____	MINSKOFF, E., Ph.D.	Teaching Approach for Developing Nonverbal Communication Skills in Students with Social Perception Deficits (Parts 1 & 2)	2.00	_____

SPANISH

QUANTITY	AUTHOR	PUBLICATION	PRICE EACH	TOTAL
_____	ACADEMIC THERAPY	Dear Parent	50	_____
_____	NAT'L. COMM. FOR CITIZENS IN EDUCATION	Set of Seven Pamphlets: Parent's Rights, School Record Rights, Suspension/Due Process Involvement in Public Schools, Consider an Appeal, How to Appeal, IEP	3.00	_____

SPELLING

QUANTITY	AUTHOR	PUBLICATION	PRICE EACH	TOTAL
_____	LAURITA, R.	Spelling as a Categorical Act	1.50	_____
_____	MORRISON, M.L.	WORD FINDER	11.95	_____

TEACHERS

QUANTITY	AUTHOR	PUBLICATION	PRICE EACH	TOTAL
_____	ADELMAN, H./TAYLOR, L.	An Introduction to Learning Disabilities	33.99	_____
_____	ACLD	L.D. in the High School: A Method Booklet for Secondary Special Subject Teachers	2.00	_____
_____	ACLD-SECONDARY COMM.	Learning Disabilities Materials Guide - Secondary Level	3.00	_____
_____	ARENA, J.	How to Write an IEP (revised 1989)	8.00	_____
_____	ARENA, J.	Teaching Educationally Handicapped	3.50	_____
_____	ARENA, J.	Teaching Through Sensor Motor Experience	5.25	_____
_____	AYRES, J.	Deficits in Sensory Integration in Educationally Handicapped Children	1.00	_____
_____	AYRES, J.	Effect of Sensory Integrative Therapy on the Coordination of Children with Choreoathetoid Movements	75	_____
_____	BANAS, N.	WISC-R Prescriptions	8.00	_____
_____	BATEMAN, B.	Three Approaches to Diagnosis & Education Planning for Children with L.D.	1.00	_____
_____	BICKART/DONOHUE/ GORNICK/GRASSI/PETERS/ ROWAN	How to Live 'Til Friday (A Handbook of practical teaching strategies for use in any classroom)	10.50	_____
_____	BROADHURST, D.	Educators, Schools and Child Abuse	3.50	_____
_____	CARROLL	Many Faces of Reading	3.00	_____
_____	CASEBEER, B.	Using the Right/Left Brain	7.00	_____
_____	COWIN/GRAFF	Comprehensive Treatment of the Older Disabled Reader	3.25	_____
_____	CRUICKSHANK, W.	Misfits in the Public Schools	5.00	_____

TEACHERS (cont.)

QUANTITY	AUTHOR	PUBLICATION	PRICE EACH	TOTAL
_____	CRUICKSHANK/MORSE/ JOHNS	Learning Disabilities, The Struggle from Adolescence Toward Adulthood	18 00	_____
_____	CRUICKSHANK, W.	The Preparation of Teachers of Brain-Injured Children	5 00	_____
_____	DANIELS, P.R.	Teaching the Gifted/Learning Disabled Child	36 00	_____
_____	DAVIS	Typing Keys	10 00	_____
_____	DOUGLAS, J.	Don't Drown in the Mainstream	6 50	_____
_____	EDWARDS, P.	Reading Problems (Identification and Treatment)	14 50	_____
_____	GAPPA/GLYNN	Room to Grow (Creating and Managing the Self-Contained Special Ed. Class)	6 95	_____
_____	GILES/KOVITZ	Helping Learning Disabled Music Students	75	_____
_____	GOLICK, M.	Playing with Words	12 95	_____
_____	HALLAHAN, D./ KAUFFMAN, J./LLOYD, J.	Introduction to Learning Disabilities	33 50	_____
_____	HAMMILL & BARTEL	Teaching Students with Learning Behavior Problems	32 00	_____
_____	HARRIS/YOST	Elements of Handwriting, A Teacher's Guide	7 00	_____
_____	JOHNSON, D.J.	Educational Principles for Children with L.D.	1 50	_____
_____	JORDON, B.T.	Perspective in L.D.	5 00	_____
_____	KEOGH, B.K.	A System of Marker Variables for the Field of Learning Disabilities	5 00	_____
_____	KIRK, S./CHALFANT, T.J.	Academic and Developmental Learning Disabilities	28 95	_____
_____	KIRK/KIRK/MINSKOFF, E.	Phonic Remedial Reading Lessons	15 00	_____
_____	KIRSCHNER, A.	Remediation of Reversals	20 00	_____
_____	KRONICK, D./SMITH, C.	Toward Productive Living	6 50	_____
_____	LAWRENCE J./STEED D./ YOUNG P.	Disruptive Children, Disruptive Schools	27 50	_____
_____	LERNER, J.	Learning Disabilities Theories, Diagnosis and Teaching Strategies	41 99	_____
_____	LIEBERMAN, L.M., Ed.D.	Special Educator's Guide	11 95	_____
_____	LIEBERMAN, L.M., Ed.D.	Preserving Special Education	11 95	_____
_____	LIEBERMAN, L.	Preventing Special Education	9 95	_____
_____	LIFSON, A.	Taming the Tornado in Your Classroom and at Home	9 75	_____
_____	LEVY, H.	Square Pegs, Round Holes (L.D. Child-Classroom & Home) (Paperback)	10 00	_____
_____	LYMAN, D.E.	Making the Words Stand Still (Paperback)	10 00	_____
_____	MAUSER, A.	Assessing the Learning Disabled: Selected Instruments	20 00	_____
_____	MUTTI/STERLING/SPALDING	Q.N.S.T. (Quick Neurological Screening Test)	12 00	_____
		Scoring Forms	10 00	_____
_____	NOYES	Fun & Fundamentals in the Classroom	3 00	_____
_____	PASTOREK, S.	Caps, Commas, and Other Things	18 00	_____
_____	PERECKE/SCHREINER	Schooling for the Learning Disabled	9 95	_____
_____	PHELPS/TERASAK/PHELPS	Teaching Written Expression	12 00	_____
_____	RAIM, J.	Case Reports in Reading and Learning Disabilities	17 75	_____
_____	RAPPAPORT, S.R.	Public Education for Children with Brain Dysfunction	5 00	_____
_____	RICKEK, LIST & LERNER	Reading Problems: Assessment and Teaching Strategies	35 00	_____
_____	ROFFMAN, A.J.	The Classroom Teacher's Guide to Mainstreaming	19 50	_____
_____	ROTALO, S.	Right-Brain Lesson Plans for a Left-Brain World	17 00	_____
_____	SAPIR, S./CORT, R.	Children with Special Needs	28 00	_____
_____	SCHLOSS & SEDLAK	Instructional Methods for Students with Learning & Behavior Problems	38 00	_____
_____	SCHOOL/COOPER	The IEP Primer	8 00	_____
_____	SIEGEL, E.	Creating Instructional Sequences	10 00	_____
_____	SEIGEL, E./GOLD, R.	Educating the Learning Disabled	30 00	_____
_____	STEVENS, S.	Classroom Success for the L.D.	10 50	_____
_____	STEVENS, S.	Enabling Disorganized Students to Succeed	5 00	_____
_____	STEWART, L.	Help for the Learning Disabled Child - Symptoms and Solutions	16 00	_____
_____	UNDERLEIDER, D.F.	Reading, Writing and RAGE	16 95	_____
_____	VITALE, B.	Unicorns Are Real: A Right-Brained Approach to Learning	13 95	_____
_____	WALLACE & LARSEN	Educational Assessment of Learning Problems: Testing for Teaching	34 00	_____
_____	WARNER, J.M.	Learning Disabilities: Activities for Remediation	8 50	_____
_____	WEISS, H. & M.	The Survival Manual: Case Studies & Suggestions for L.D. Teens	9 75	_____
_____	YOUNG & SAVAGE	How to Help Students Overcome Learning Problems & LD (2nd Edition)	23 00	_____

VISUAL

QUANTITY	AUTHOR	PUBLICATION	PRICE EACH	TOTAL
_____	FLAX, N., O.D.	The Contribution of Visual Problems to Learning Disabilities	1 50	_____
_____	FLAX, N., O.D.	Strictly for Parents/Visual Function in Learning Disabilities	1 50	_____
_____	FLAX, N., O.D.	Vision and Learning Disabilities: Optometry's Contribution	2 25	_____
_____	PEISER, I.	Vision and Learning Disabilities	1 25	_____

VOCATIONAL

QUANTITY	AUTHOR	PUBLICATION	EACH	TOTAL
_____	BILLER, F.E.	Understanding Adolescents and Young Adults with Learning Disabilities: A Focus on Employability and Career Placement	22.00	_____
_____	BILLER, F.E.	Understanding & Guiding the Career Development of Adolescents and Young Adults with L.D.	23.00	_____
_____	SMITH/BERENSON/SMITH	Career Planner: A Guide for Students with Disabilities	4.00	_____
_____	WASHBURN, W.	Vocational Entry Skills for Secondary Students	13.00	_____
_____	WASHBURN, W.	1 Set Worksheets	7.00	_____

NEW ADDITIONS

QUANTITY	AUTHOR	PUBLICATION	EACH	TOTAL
_____	RICH, D.	Mega-Skills - How Families Can Help Children Succeed in School and Beyond	10.00	_____
_____	MULTILINGUAL ELEM.			
_____	TRUCH, S.	The WISC-R Companion	45.00	_____
_____	MOSS, P. BUCKLEY	P. Buckley Moss - The People's Artist, An Autobiography	12.00	_____
_____	LDA	Learning Disabilities: A Multidisciplinary Journal (Single Copy)	13.00	_____
_____	BARTOLI/BOTEL	Reading/Learning Disability An Ecological Approach	19.00	_____
_____	GOLDEN EMPIRE HEALTH PLANNING CENTER	Toxics in My Home? Curriculum on Household Toxics for Grades 9-12	14.00	_____
_____	JOHNSON/ROSE/WINDELL	Stress and You - A Guide to Better Living	3.00	_____
_____	JOHNSON, R./BLALOCK, J.	Adults with Learning Disabilities / Clinical Studies	36.00	_____
_____	KRUGER SMITH, B.	Learning Disabilities in the Future: LD in AD 2000	2.00	_____
_____	CAVEY, D.	Dysgraphia: Why Johnny Can't Write	7.00	_____
_____	VAUGHN/BOS	Research in Learning Disabilities: Issues and Future Directions	30.00	_____
_____	RYNDERS, P., Ph.D.	The Hidden Problem - A Guide to Solving the Problem of Illiteracy	3.00	_____
_____	CORDONI, B.	Living with a Learning Disability	15.95	_____
_____	LEVINE, M., M.D.	Developmental Variation and Learning Disorders	49.99	_____
_____	SILVER, R.A., Ed.D.	Art as Language for the LD Child	1.00	_____
_____	SMITH, SALLY	Masking the Feeling of Being Stupid	2.00	_____
_____	LDA OF CANADA	The Three R's - Rights / Routes / Responsibilities	4.00	_____
_____	MAHONEY/RESNICK	Please Doctor - If someone should mention learning disabilities	4.50	_____
_____	WILLIG/GREENBERG	Bilingualism and Learning Disabilities	19.50	_____
_____	TABER, F.	Microcomputers in Special Education	8.50	_____
_____	SILVER, L.	The Assessment of Learning Disabilities	29.00	_____
_____	SZATMARI/BARTOLUCCI/ BRENNER/BOND/RICH	A Follow-Up Study of High-Functioning Autistic Children	3.00	_____
_____	RIPLEY/CVACH	Recreation for Children with Learning Disabilities	2.00	_____
_____	WARNER, C.	Understanding Your Learning Disability	3.00	_____
_____	ANDERSON/CHITWOOD/ HAYDEN	Negotiating the Special Education Maze: A Guide for Parents and Teachers	12.95	_____
_____	MARCH OF DIMES	Research in Infant Assessment	22.00	_____
_____	LEKOTEK	1989/90 Innotek Resource Guide: A Guide for Selecting Software for Children with Special Needs (LD Programs specifically identified)	20.00	_____
_____	SILVER, L.	Psychological and Family Problems Associated with Learning Disabilities: Assessment and Intervention	1.00	_____
_____	KAVANAGH, J./TRUSS, T.	Learning Disabilities: Proceedings of the National Conference	3.00	_____
_____	GARENTT, K./GERBER, P.	Life Transitions of Learning Disabled Adults: Perspectives from Several Countries	4.50	_____
_____	GAMSBY, L.	Coping with School: Organizational and Learning Techniques for Parents, Teachers and Students	7.50	_____
_____	BALLARD/RAMIREZ/ ZANTAL-WEINER	Public Law 94-142, Section 504, and Public Law 99-457: Understanding What They Are and Are Not	3.50	_____
_____	MALL, M., MD	An Introduction to Your Child Who Has ASTHMA	2.50	_____
_____	STEVENS, S.	How to Rescue At-Risk Students - A Teacher's Guide	8.25	_____
_____	HAAD	How to Own and Operate An Attention Deficit Kid	6.00	_____
_____	BLOOM, M.	Help Me to Help My Child - A Sourcebook for Parents of Learning Disabled Children	19.00	_____
_____	MARIA, K.	Reading Comprehension Instruction: Issues & Strategies (1990)	27.00	_____
_____	LEVINE, DR. M.	Keeping a Head in School - A Student's Book About Learning Abilities and Learning Disorders	16.50	_____
_____	SWANSON, H./KEOGH, B.	Learning Disabilities - Theoretical and Research Issues (A review and critique of research in the areas of intellignece, social congnition, achievement, and subtyping as they relate to learning disabilities)	55.95	_____
_____	SWANSON, H.	Handbook on the Assessment of Learning Disabilities - Theory, Research, and Practice	37.00	_____
_____	DIAS, P.S.	Diamonds in the Rough - An Infancy to College Reference Guide on the Learning Disabled Child	22.00	_____
_____	TRAPANI, C., PH.D.	Transition Goals for Adolescents with LD (1990)	25.50	_____

QUANTITY	AUTHOR	PUBLICATION	PRICE EACH	TOTAL

NEW ADDITIONS (cont.)

QUANTITY	AUTHOR	PUBLICATION	PRICE EACH	TOTAL
_____	ALLEN, R.J., PH.D.	Developing and Remediating Perceptual Skills for Learning Disabled Children in the Primary Grades (1990)	7.50	_____
_____	TAYLOR, J.F.	Helping Your Hyperactive Child - From Effective Treatments and Developing Discipline and Self-Esteem to Helping Your Family Adjust (1990)	20.00	_____
_____	LANDI, P.C.	Parenting Attention Deficit Disordered Teens (1990)	3.50	_____
_____	HARWELL, J.M.	Complete Learning Disabilities Handbook - Ready-to-Use Techniques for Teaching Learning Handicapped Students (1989)	28.00	_____
_____	LUTZ, L./POLLAK, P.	Basic Math Skills: A Handbook for Tutors (1982)	7.00	_____
_____	WOODS, J.	How to Succeed in College with Dyslexia (1989)	18.95	_____
_____	FISHER, G./ CUMMINGS, R.	The Survival Guide for Kids with LD (Learning Differences) (1990)	9.95	_____
_____	LDA OF CANADA	Job Interview Tips for People with Learning Disabilities (1990)	17.00	_____
_____	LDA OF CANADA	Help Build a Brighter Future - Identification of Children at Risk for Learning Disabilities in Child Care Centers (1990)	8.00	_____
_____	LIGHT, H./MORRISON, P.	Beyond Retention - A Survival Guide for Regular Classroom Teachers (1990)	15.00	_____
_____	JOHNSON, D.	School-Physician Collaboration for the Student with Attentional Difficulties: Handbook for Intervention (1989)	10.00	_____
_____	TORGESEN, J.	Cognitive and Behavioral Characteristics of Children with Learning Disabilities (1990)	26.00	_____
_____	HOWARD, D.	Swimming Upstream - A Complete Guide to the College Application Process for the Learning Disabled Student (1988)	22.99	_____
_____	FOWLER, M.	Maybe You Know My Kid - A Parent's Guide to Identifying, Understanding and Helping Your Child with Attention-Deficit Hyperactivity Disorder (1990)	18.95	_____
_____	ORLOW, M.	A Student's Guide to Good Grades (1990)	14.00	_____
_____	BATEMAN, B.	So You're Going to Hearing - Preparing for a Public Law 94-142 Due Process Hearing (1980)	5.50	_____
_____	COMINGS, D.	Tourette Syndrome & Human Behavior (1990)	39.95	_____
_____	HEALY, J.	Endangered Minds: Why our Children Don't Think (1990) Thoughtful and provacative, this offers much to parents regarding the development of their children's reading and critical thinking abilities.	23.95	_____
_____	WALLBROWN/WALLBROWN	So Your Child Has a Learning Problem: Now What? (revised 1990) Provides parents with information necessary to help them ask the "right questions" in their dealings with professionals.	21.95	_____
_____	GOTTESMAN, CERULLO, NATHAN	Helping the Child with Learning Disabilities: A SCHOOL VOLUNTEER'S GUIDE	5.00	_____

VCR TAPES

QUANTITY	PUBLICATION	PRICE EACH	TOTAL
_____	*I'm Not Stupid* - This video depicts the constant battle of the learning disabled child in school. It points out how the LD child is often misdiagnosed as slow, retarded, emotionally disturbed, or even just a lazy kid. This highly recommended documentary is for parents, teachers, administrators, students or anyone who wants to learn what it is like to live with learning disabilities. (53 minutes)	22.00	_____
_____	*All Children Learn Differently* - Narrated by Steve Allen, this video interviews 12 specialists in medicine, perception, language and education. It takes a nutritional/educational approach to the remediation of learning disabilities, calling for the "right professional team" for each child. (30 minutes)	39.95	_____

- -

NAME: _____

ADDRESS: _____

CITY: _____ STATE: _____ ZIP: _____

ALL ORDERS MUST BE PREPAID   **NO REFUNDS**   **PLEASE PRINT ABOVE INFORMATION**

SEND ORDER TO:
LDA
LITERARY DEPOSITORY
4156 Library Road
Pittsburgh, PA 15234

SUB TOTAL _____

10% POSTAGE/HANDLING _____
($1.00 minimum)
TOTAL U.S. CURRENCY _____

Glossary of Learning Disabilities Terms

This glossary is a compilation of terms and definitions adapted from a number of sources, which are duly noted. All definitions not otherwise attributed have been written by the Learning Disabilities Council's Handbook Writing Committee.

A separate glossary, specifically describing educational tests, follows this glossary.

Academic Classes - Classes in basic subjects such as reading, arithmetic, science, and social studies at elementary level; and English, history, science, and math at secondary level.(1)

Achievement Test - A test that measures the extent to which a person has acquired certain information or mastered certain skills, usually as a result of planned instruction or training. These tests are often called educational tests.

Adaptive Physical Education - A special physical education program developed to fit the limits and disabilities of persons with handicaps.(2)

Amphetamines - A group of drugs used to stimulate the cerebral cortex of the brain. Sometimes used to treat hyperactivity. (*See also* Dexedrine and Ritalin.)(2)

Anoxia - Deficient amount of oxygen in the tissues of a part of the body or in the bloodstream supplying such part.(3)

Aptitude Test - A test designed to measure a person's ability to learn and the likelihood of success in future school work or in a specific career.

Articulation (Speech) - Refers to the production of speech sounds resulting from the movements of the lips, jaw, and tongue as they modify the flow of air.(1)

Association - Ability to relate concepts presented through the senses (visual, auditory, tactile, or kinesthetic).(4)

Attention Deficit Disorders (ADD) - A term frequently used to describe the academic and behavioral problems of children who have difficulty focusing and maintaining attention. Also called Attention Deficit Hyperactivity Disorders (ADHD).

Attention Span - The length of time an individual can concentrate on a task without being distracted or losing interest. (*See also* Distractability.)(2)

Auditory Discrimination - Ability to detect differences in sounds; may be gross ability, such as detecting the differences between the noises made by a cat and dog, or fine ability, such as detecting the differences made by the sounds of letters "m" and "n."

Auditory Figure-Ground - Ability to attend to one sound against a background of sound (e.g., hearing the teacher's voice against classroom noise).(5)

Auditory Memory - Ability to retain information which has been presented orally; may be short term memory, such as recalling information presented several seconds before; long term memory, such as recalling information presented more than a minute before; or sequential memory, such as recalling a series of information in proper order.

Basic Skill Area - Includes such subjects as reading, writing, spelling, mathematics.(1)

Behavior Modification - A technique intended to change behavior by rewarding desirable actions and ignoring or "negatively rewarding" undesirable actions.(2)

Binocular Fusion - The blending of separate images from each eye into a single meaningful image.(2)

Blending - *See* Sound Blending.(1)

Body Image - The concept and awareness of one's own body as it relates to space, movement, and other objects.(5)

Brain Damage - Any actual structural (tissue) damage due to any cause or causes. This means verifiable damage, not neurological performance that is indicative of damage.

Catastrophic Reaction - Extreme terror, grief, frustration, or anger without apparent cause. May be triggered by changes in routine, unexpected events, or over stimulation. Children reacting in this manner may throw or break things, scream uncontrollably, or burst into tears.(2)

CEC - Council for Exceptional Children.(2)

Central Nervous System (CNS) - The brain and spinal cord.(2)

Cerebral Cortex - The outer layer of the brain; controls thinking, feeling, and voluntary movement.(2)

Channel - The routes through which the content of communication flows. It includes both the modalities through which impression is received and the form of expression through which the response is made. Ex: Auditory—Vocal Channel.(4)

Child Study Committee - Is located in each school building to receive and act upon referrals of students suspected of being handicapped. The membership of this committee usually consists of at least three persons, including the school principal or a person chosen by the principal, the teacher or teachers, specialists, and the referring source if appropriate.

CNS - *See* Central Nervous System.(2)

Cognition - The act or process of knowing; the various thinking skills and processes are considered cognitive skills.(7)

Cognitive Ability - Intellectual ability; thinking and reasoning skills.

Cognitive Style - A person's typical approach to learning activities and problem solving. For example, some people carefully analyze each task, deciding what must be done and in what order. Others react impulsively to situations.(2)

Compensation - Process in which a person is taught how to cope with his learning problems, how to "work around" skills or abilities which may be lacking; emphasis is placed on using the individual's strengths. (*See* Remediation.)

Conceptualization - The process of forming a general idea from what is observed. For example, seeing apples, bananas, and oranges and recognizing that they are all fruit.(2)

Conceptual Disorder - Disturbances in thinking, reasoning, generalizing, memorizing.

Confidential File - File maintained by the school; contains evaluations conducted to determine whether a child is handicapped, as well as any other information related to special education placement. This is a "limited access" file; however, parents do have a right to inspect the file and have copies of any information contained in it.

Configuration - The visual shape or form of words; may be used as a cue in word-attack skills.(8)

Congenital - A condition existing at birth or before birth. Congenital does not imply that a condition is hereditary.(2)

Coordination - The harmonious functioning of muscles in the body to perform complex movements.(2)

Criterion Referenced Test - Designed to provide information on specific knowledge or skills possessed by a student. Such tests usually cover relatively small units of content and are closely related to instruction. Their scores have meaning in terms of what the student knows or can do, rather than their relation to the scores made by some external reference group.

Cross-Categorical - Refers to a system in which a teacher addresses more than one handicapping condition within one instructional period.(1)

Cross Dominance - A condition in which the preferred eye, hand, or foot are not on the same side of the body. For example, a person may be right-footed and right-eyed but left-handed. Also called mixed dominance.(2)

Cumulative File - General file maintained by the school for any child enrolled in the school. Parents have a right to inspect the file and have copies of any information contained in it.

Decoding - The process of getting meaning from written or spoken symbols. (*See* Receptive Language.)(2)

Developmental Lag - A delay in some aspect of physical or mental development.(2)

Dexedrine - Trade name for one of several stimulant drugs often given to modify hyperactivity in children.(2)

Directionality - The ability to know right from left, up from down, forward from backward, and direction and orientation.(9)

Discrepancy - Significant difference.

Discrimination - Process of detecting differences between and/or among stimuli.(1)

Disinhibition - Lack of restraint in responding to a situation. A child exhibiting disinhibition reacts impulsively and often inappropriately.(2)

Distractibility - The shifting of attention from the task at hand to sounds, sights, and other stimuli that normally occur in the environment.(2)

Due Process - The application of law to ensure that an individual's rights are protected. When applied to children with learning disabilities, due process means that parents have the right to request a full review of any educational program developed for their child. A due process hearing may be requested to ensure that all requirements of Public Law 94-142 have been met.(2)

Dysarthria - A disorder of the speech muscles that affects the ability to pronounce words.(2)

Dyscalculia - Difficulty in understanding or using mathematical symbols or functions. A child with dyscalculia may be able to read and write but have difficulty in performing mathematical calculations.

Dysfunction - Any disturbance or impairment in the normal functioning of an organ or body part.(2)

Dysgraphia - Difficulty in producing legible handwriting with age-appropriate speed.

Dyslexia - Impairment of the ability to deal with language (speaking, reading, spelling, writing). A dyslexic may "see" letters, syllables, or words upside down, reversed, blurred, backwards, or otherwise distorted.

Dysnomia - Difficulty in remembering names or recalling appropriate words to use in a given context.

Dyspraxia - Difficulty in performing fine motor acts such as drawing, buttoning, etc. A person with dyspraxia has difficulty producing and sequencing the movements necessary to perform these kinds of tasks.

Early Intervention Program - A program specially designed to assist developmentally delayed infants and preschool children. The purpose of this type of program is to help prevent problems as the child matures.(2)

Educational Consultant/Diagnostician - An individual who may be familiar with school curriculum and requirements at various grade levels; may or may not have a background in learning disabilities; may conduct educational evaluations.

Educational Evaluation - One of the components necessary to determine whether a child is handicapped. Although the specific content of an educational evaluation is not specified by the regulations, the evaluation generally consists of a battery of tests and/or classroom observation and analysis of class work designed to determine the current levels of achievement in areas such as reading, math, spelling, etc. Perceptual abilities and learning style may also be evaluated.

Educational Psychologist - *See* School Psychologist.

Electroencephalogram (EEG) - A graphic recording of electrical currents developed in the cerebral cortex during brain functioning. Sometimes called a "brain wave test." A machine called an electroencephalograph records the pattern of these electrical currents on paper.(2)

Eligibility Committee - Determines (1) whether a child has a handicapping condition which requires special education and, in some cases, related services such as speech and language therapy; (2) identifies the handicapping condition and recommends the special education services (and, where needed, related services) that are needed. It is composed of the special education administrator or a person representing the administrator and school division personnel representative of the disciplines involved in the conduct of the evaluation (e.g., psychologist, educational diagnostician). At least one school division representative must be a person who tested or observed the student.

Encoding - The process of expressing language (i.e., selecting words; formulating them into ideas; producing them through speaking or writing). (*See* Expressive Language.)(1)

Etiology - The study of the cause or origin of a condition or disease.(2)

Expressive Language - Communication through writing, speaking, and/or gestures.(2)

Eye-Hand Coordination - The ability of the eyes and hands to work together to complete a task. Examples are drawing and writing.(2)

Far Point Copying - Writing while copying from a model some distance away, e.g., copying from the blackboard.

FCLD - Foundation for Children with Learning Disabilities.(2) (Now known as NCLD—The National Center for Learning Disabilities.)

Figure-Ground Discrimination - The ability to sort out important information from the surrounding environment. For example, hearing a teacher's voice while ignoring other classroom noises (air conditioners, heaters, etc.) or seeing a word among others on a crowded page.(2)

Fine Motor - The use of small muscles for precision tasks such as writing, tying bows, zipping a zipper, typing, doing puzzles.(2)

General Education - All education not included under Special Education. (*See* Regular Education.)(1)

Gross Motor - The use of large muscles for activities requiring strength and balance. Examples are walking, running, and jumping.(2)

Handicapped - Any person with any physical and/or mental disability who has difficulty in doing certain tasks such as walking, seeing, hearing, speaking, learning, or working. Federal law defines handicapped children as those who are "mentally retarded, hard of hearing, deaf, speech impaired, visually handicapped, seriously emotionally disturbed, orthopedically impaired, other health impaired, blind, multihandicapped, or as having specific learning disabilities" and who require special educational services because of these disabilities.(2)

Haptic Sense - Combined kinesthetic and tactile sense.(1)

Hyperkinesis - Another term for hyperactivity.(1)

Hyperactivity (or Hyperkinesis) - Disorganized and disruptive behavior characterized by constant and excessive movement. A hyperactive child usually has difficulty sticking to one task for an extended period and may react more intensely to a situation than a normal child.(2)

Hypoactivity - Underactivity; child may appear to be in a daze, lacking energy.

IEP - *See* Individualized Education Plan (or Program).

IEP Committee - Writes the Individualized Education Program for the youngster who has been identified by the Eligibility Committee as handicapped. Members are (1) a school division employee, other than the student's teacher, who is qualified to provide or supervise special education; (2) the student's teacher(s); (3) the parent or guardian; (4) the student, if appropriate; (5) other individuals whom the parents or the school division select.

Impulsivity - Reacting to a situation without considering the consequences.(2)

Individualized Education Plan (IEP) - A written educational prescription developed for each handicapped (including learning disabled) child. Sometimes called an Individualized Education Program. School districts are required by law to develop these plans, in cooperation with parents. An IEP must contain:
  – the child's present levels of educational performance
  – annual and short-term educational goals
  – the specific special education program and related services that will be provided to the child
  – the extent to which the child will participate in regular education program with non-handicapped children
  – a statement of when services will begin and how long they will last
  – provisions for evaluating the effectiveness of the program and the student's performance. This evaluation must occur at least once a year.
  – statement of transition services for students 14 years of age or older.(2)

Informal Tests - Task-oriented tests to provide information concerning specific skills. Are not standardized.(1)

Integrity - Complete, unimpaired.(8)

Insertions - In reading, spelling, or math, the addition of letters or numbers which do not belong in a word or numeral, e.g., "sinceare" for "sincere."

Inversions - In reading, spelling, or math, confusion of up-down directionality of letters or numbers, e.g., m for w, 6 for 9, etc.

IQ - Intelligence quotient. The ratio between a person's chronological age (measured in years) and mental age (as measured by an intelligence test), multiplied by 100.(2)

Itinerant Teacher - Special Education teacher who is shared by more than one school.(8)

Kinesthetic - Pertaining to the muscles.(2)

Kinesthetic Method - A way of teaching words by using the muscles. For example, a student might trace the outline of a word with a finger while looking at the word and saying aloud the word or its letters, in sequence.(2)

Laterality - The tendency to use the hand, foot, eye, and ear on a particular side of the body. For example, many people use their right hand when eating and their right foot when kicking.(2)

LD - Learning disability, learning disabled, learning disabilities.(2)

LDAA - Learning Disabiliites Association of America.

LEA - Local Education Agency (a school division).

Learning Disabilities (LD) - Disorders of the basic psychological processes that affect the way a child learns. Many children with learning disabilities have average or above average intelligence. Learning disabilities may cause difficulties in listening, thinking, talking, reading, writing, spelling, or arithmetic. Included are perceptual handicaps, dyslexia, and developmental aphasia. Excluded are learning difficulties caused by visual, hearing, or motor handicaps, mental retardation, emotional disturbances, or environmental disadvantage.(2)

Learning Disorder - Damage or impairment to the nervous system that results in a learning disability.(2)

Learning Style - The channels through which a person best understands and retains learning. All individuals learn best through one or more channels: vision, hearing, movement, touching, or a combination of these.

Lesion- Abnormal change in body tissue due to injury or disease.(2)

Licensed Clinical Psychologist - A psychologist who is competent to apply the principles and techniques of psychological evaluation and psychotherapy to individual clients for the purpose of ameliorating problems of behavioral and/or emotional maladjustment.(12)

Licensed Clinical Social Worker - A social worker who, by education and experience, is professionally qualified to provide direct diagnostic, preventive and treatment services where functioning is threatened or affected by social and psychological stress or health impairment.(12)

Licensed Professional Counselor - A person trained in counseling and guidance services with emphasis on individual and group guidance and counseling; assists individuals in achieving more effective personal, social, educational, and career development and adjustment.(12)

Linguistic Approach - Method for teaching reading (decoding skills) which emphasizes use of "word families." For example, the child is taught to read "at" and then subsequently is taught to decode words such as "cat," "bat," "sat," "mat," etc. Early stories adhere strictly to the words which have been taught previously and so may sometimes seem nonsensical,e.g., "Sam sat on a mat. The cat sat on a mat. The cat is fat," etc.

Mainstreaming - The practice of placing handicapped children with special educational needs into regular classrooms for at least a part of the children's school programs.(2)

Maturation Lag - Delayed maturity in one or several skills or areas of development.(2)

Mental Age - The age for which a given score on a mental ability test is average or normal. The term is most appropriately used at the early age levels where mental growth is rapid.(8)

Milieu Therapy - A clinical technique designed to control a child's environment and minimize conflicting and confusing information.(2)

Minimal Brain Dysfunction (MBD) - A broad and unspecific term formerly used to describe learning disabilities.(2)

Mixed Dominance - *See* cross dominance.(2)

Mixed Laterality or Lateral Confusion - Tendency to perform some acts with a right side preference and others with a left, or the shifting from right to left for certain activities.(10)

Modality - The sensory channel used to acquire information. Visual, auditory, tactile, kinesthetic, olfactory (odors), and gustatory (taste) are the most common modalities.(2)

Modified Self-Contained - Closely approximates the self-contained class; however, students receive instruction from a regular education teacher for some part of the school day.(1)

Motor - Pertaining to the origin or execution of muscular activity.(3)

Multi-Categorical - A special education classroom model in which students with more than one handicapping condition are assigned to a special education teacher.(1)

Multidisciplinary Team - In education, a group made up of a child's classroom teacher and several educational specialists that evaluates the child's handicap and prepares an Individualized Education Plan for the child.(2)

Multisensory - Involving most or all of the senses.(2)

NCLD - National Center for Learning Disabilities.

Near Point Copying- Writing while copying from a model close at hand, e.g., copying from a textbook.

Neurological Examination - Testing of the sensory or motor responses to determine if there is impairment of the nervous system.(2)

Noncategorical - Refers to a system of grouping handicapped children together without reference to a particular label or category of exceptionality.(7)

Norm-Referenced Test - *See* Standardized Test.(2)

Norms - Statistics that provide a frame of reference by which meaning may be given to test scores. Norms are based upon the actual performance of pupils of various grades or ages in the standardization group for the test. Since they represent average or typical performance, they should not be regarded as standards or universally desirable levels of attainment. The most common types of norms are standard scores such as stanines or deviation IQ, percentile rank, grade or age equivalents.

Ombudsman - An official appointed to investigate complaints and speak for individuals with grievances.(2)

Oral Language - Those verbal communication skills needed to understand (listen) and to use (speak) language.

Organicity - A disorder of the central nervous system; brain damage.(2)

Orton Dyslexia Society - Organization of professionals in the field of LD as well as scientists and parents.

Orton-Gillingham Approach - An approach to teaching individuals with learning disabilities. The technique, devised by Dr. Samuel Orton, Anna Gillingham, and Bessie Stillman, stresses a multisensory, phonetic, structured, sequential approach to learning.

Perceptual Abilities - The abilities to process, organize, and interpret the information obtained by the five senses; a function of the brain.

Perceptual Handicap - Difficulty in ability to process and organize as well as interpret information through the senses.

Perceptual-Motor - Muscle activity resulting from information received through the senses.(2)

Perceptual Speed - Specific meaning of this term varies, depending upon the manner in which a given test measures this ability. May refer to motor speed, how fast something is copied or manipulated, or to visual discrimination, e.g., how quickly identical items in a given series are identified, etc.

Perseveration - The repeating of words, motions, or tasks. A child who perseverates often has difficulty shifting to a new task and continues working on an old task long after classmates have stopped.(2)

Phonics Approach - Method for teaching reading and spelling in which emphasis is placed on learning the sounds which individual and various combinations of letters make in a word. In decoding a word, the child sounds out individual letters or letter combinations and then blends them to form a word.

Psychiatrist - An individual who treats behavioral or emotional problems. Is a licensed medical doctor (M.D.), so is permitted to use medications in treating a problem.

Psychological Examination - An evaluation by a certified school or clinical psychologist of the intellectual and behavioral characteristics of a person. (1)

Psychomotor - Pertaining to the motor effects of psychological processes. Psychomotor tests are tests of motor skill which depend upon sensory or perceptual motor coordination. (3)

Public Law (P.L.) 94-142 - The federal Education for All Handicapped Children Act that became law in 1975. P.L. 94-142 requires each state to provide free and appropriate public education to all handicapped children from birth through age 21. The law also requires that an Individualized Education Plan be prepared for each handicapped child, that parents must have access to their child's school records, and are entitled to a due process hearing if they are dissatisfied with the educational plan.(2)

Readiness - Acquisition of skills considered prerequisite for academic learning.(8)

Reasoning Ability - Specific meaning of this term varies, depending upon the manner in which a given test measures this ability; generally refers to nonverbal, deductive, inductive, analytical thinking.

Receptive Language (Decoding) - Language that is spoken or written by others and received by the individual. The receptive language skills are listening and reading.(7)

Regrouping- In arithmetic, the processes traditionally known as "carrying" in addition or "borrowing" in subtraction.

Regular Education - All education not included under Special Education (*see* General Education).(1)

Rehabilitation Act of 1973 - The Civil Rights Act for the Handicapped. The act prohibits discrimination on the basis of physical or mental handicap in all federally-assisted programs. Section 504 of the act stipulates that handicapped people are entitled to:
- the same rights and benefits as non-handicapped applicants and employees
- all medical services and medically-related instruction available to the public
- participate in vocational rehabilitation, senior citizen activities, day care (for disabled children), or any other social service program receiving federal assistance on an equal basis with nonhandicapped persons
- an appropriate elementary and secondary education for physically or mentally handicapped children. (2)

Remediation - Process in which an individual is provided instruction and practice in skills which are weak or nonexistent in an effort to develop/strengthen these skills.

Resource Room - An instructional setting to which a special education student goes for specified periods of time on a regularly scheduled basis.(1)

Resource Teacher - A specialist who works with handicapped students; may also act as a consultant to other teachers.(1)

Reversals- Difficulty in reading or reproducing letters alone, letters in words, or words in sentences in their proper position in space or in proper order. May also refer to reversal of mathematical concepts (add/subtract, multiply/divide) and symbols (><; x+). *See also* Transposition.(1)

Ritalin - Trade name for one of several stimulant drugs often given to modify hyperactivity in children.(2)

Scatter - Variability in an individual's test scores.(11)

School Psychologist - A person who specializes in problems manifested in and associated with educational systems and who uses psychological concepts and methods in programs which attempt to improve learning conditions for students.(12)

SEA - State Education Agency (the state Department of Education).

Self-Concept - How a person feels and thinks about himself or herself. Sometimes called self-image.(2)

Self-Contained Classroom - Special class for specific types of handicapped students who spend all or the largest portion of the school day in this setting.(1)

Semantics - The meaning or understanding given to oral or written language.

Sensorimotor - Relationship between sensation and movement. Sometimes spelled sensory-motor.(2)

Sensory Acuity - The ability to respond to sensation at normal levels of intensity.(3)

Sequence - The detail of information in its accustomed order (for example, days of the week, the alphabet, etc.).(1)

Sight Words - Words a child can recognize on sight without aid of phonics or other word-attack skills.(8)

Sight Word Approach - Also known as "whole word" approach; method for teaching reading which relies heavily upon a child's visual memory skills, with minimal emphasis on sounding out a word; child memorizes the word based on its overall configuration.

SLD - Specific learning disability. Difficulty in certain areas of learning is contrasted with a general learning disability, i.e., difficulty in all areas of learning. Learning disabilities as discussed in this handbook are SLD. (SLD is also sometimes interpreted as Specific Language Disability.)

Slingerland Method - A highly structured, multisensory teaching method designed for group instruction of persons with specific learning disabilities. Named for its developer, Beth Slingerland.(2)

Social Perceptions - The ability to interpret stimuli in the social environment and appropriately relate such interpretations to social situations.

Socio-Cultural - Combined social and cultural factors as they affect the development of a child in all areas of life.(1)

Soft Neurological Signs - Neurological abnormalities that are mild or slight and difficult to detect, as contrasted with the gross or obvious neurological abnormalities.(7)

Sound Blending - The ability to combine smoothly all the sounds or parts of a word into the whole.(8)

Spatial Orientation - Awareness of space around the person in terms of distance, form, direction, and position.(3)

Spatial Relationships - The ability to perceive the relationships between self and two or more objects and the relationships of the objects to each other.(8)

Special Education - Instruction specifically designed for handicapped children.(2)

Specific Language Disability (SLD) - Difficulty in some aspect of learning how to read, write, spell, or speak. Is also called Specific Language Learning Disability.

Standardized Test - A test that compares a child's performance with the performance of a large group of similar children (usually children of the same age). Also called a norm-referenced test. IQ tests and most achievement tests are standardized.(2)

Structure - Consistent use of rules, limits, and routines. The use of structure reassures a child with learning disabilities that the environment is somewhat predictable and stable.(2)

Structural Analysis - Using syllabication, prefix, suffix, and root word clues, etc. to read or spell a word.

Substitution - In reading, spelling, or math, interchanging a given letter, number, or word for another, e.g., "sereal" for "cereal."

Survival Skills - Minimal skills needed for a student to cope with everyday society.(1)

Syntax - Grammar, sentence structure, and word order in oral or written language.

Syndrome - A set of symptoms that indicates a specific disorder.(2)

Tactile - Having to do with the sense of touch.(2)

Task Analysis - The technique of carefully examining a particular task to discover the elements it comprises and the processes required to perform it.(7)

Thematic Maturity - Ability to write in a logical, organized manner that easily and efficiently conveys meaning.

Thinking Skills - Refers to the manner in which humans acquire, interpret, organize, store, retrieve, and employ knowledge.(1)

Transposition - In reading, spelling, or math, confusion of the order of letters in a word or numbers in a numeral, e.g., sliver for silver, 432 for 423, etc.

VAKT - Acronym for visual-auditory-kinesthetic-tactile; multisensory teaching approach which emphasizes using all of the senses to teach skills and concepts.

Verbal Ability - Specific meaning of this term varies, depending upon the manner in which a given test measures this ability. Generally refers to oral or spoken language abilities.

Visual Association - Ability to relate concepts which are presented visually, through pictures or written words. For example, given a picture of a dog, house, flower and bone, the child is able to indicate that the dog and bone go together.

Visual Closure - Ability to see only the outline of an item or picture, or a partially completed picture, and still be able to indicate what it is.

Visual Discrimination - Ability to detect similarities and/or differences in materials which are presented visually, e.g., ability to discriminate h from n, o from c, b from d, etc.

Visual Figure-Ground - Ability to focus on the foreground of material presented visually, rather than background. Those who have difficulty with this may find it hard to keep their place while copying or reading, may find a crowded page of print or illustrations confusing, etc.

Visual Memory - Ability to retain information which is presented visually; may be short term memory, such as recalling information presented several seconds before; long term memory, such as recalling information presented more than a minute before; or sequential memory, such as recalling a series of information in proper order.

Visual Motor - Ability to translate information received visually into a motor response. Difficulties are often characterized by poor handwriting, etc.

Visual Perception - Ability to correctly interpret what is seen. For example, a child sees a triangle and identifies it as a triangle.(2)

Word Attack Skills - Ability to analyze unfamiliar words visually and phonetically.(2)

Word Recognition - Ability to read or pronounce a word; usually implies that the word is recognized immediately by sight and that the child does not need to apply word analysis skills. Does not imply understanding of the word.

Written Language - Encompasses all facets of written expression, e.g., handwriting, capitalization, punctuation, spelling, format, ability to express one's thoughts in sentences and paragraphs, etc.

[1]Virginia Department of Education. (1980). *The guidelines for programs for students with specific learning disabilities in Virginia's public schools.* Richmond, VA: Author. Reprinted with permission.

[2]Foundation for Children with Learning Disabilities. (1985). *The FCLD Learning Disabilities Resource Guide.* New York: Author, 99 Park Avenue, New York, NY 10016. Founder and President, Carrie Rozelle. Reprinted with permission. pp. 382–390.

[3]Myers, P. and Hammill, D. (1976). *Methods for learning disorders,* (Second Edition). New York: John Wiley & Sons, Inc.

[4]Kirk, S. A. and Kirk, W. D. (1971). *Psycholinguistic learning disabilities: Diagnosis and remediation.* Urbana, IL: University of Illinois Press.

[5]*SLD Gazette.* (1977, March). Newton, MA: Massachusetts Association for Children and Adults with Learning Disabilities.

[6]Gerheart, W. (1977). *Learning disabilities: Educational strategies,* (Second Edition). St. Louis: C. V. Mosby Co.

[7]Lerner, J. W. (1976). *Children with learning disabilities,* (Second Edition). Boston, MA: Houghton-Mifflin Co.

[8]Wallace, G. (1975). *Characteristics of learning disabilities: A television series.* Richmond, VA: The L.D. Council.

[9]Valett, R. E. (1967). *The remediation of learning disabilities.* Palo Alto, CA: Fearon Publishers.

[10]Lerner, J. (1971). *Learning diasabilities: Theories, diagnosis and teaching strategies.* Boston: Houghton-Mifflin.

[11]Bryan, T. and Bryan, J. (1978). *Understanding learning disabilities,* (Second Edition). Sherman Oaks, CA: Alfred Pub. Co.

[12]Virginia Department of Health Regulatory Boards: *Code of Virginia, Chapter 28 - Behavioral Science Professions.* Richmond, VA: Author.

Glossary of Educational Tests[1]

I. Achievement Screening

- **Battelle Developmental Inventory** - Measures developmental levels in preschool and kindergarten children.

- **Kaufman Test of Educational Ability (KTEA)** - Appropriate for children aged 6-18 years; measures math applications and computation, reading decoding and comprehension, and spelling. A specific error analysis of skills tested is also provided. Standardized.

- **Peabody Individual Achievement Test (PIAT)** - Appropriate for children aged 5.3-18.3 years; measures mathematics, reading recognition, reading comprehension (child reads a sentence and then selects a picture to go with the sentence), spelling (child selects correctly spelled word), general information (child answers oral questions). In mathematics, reading comprehension and spelling, a multiple choice answer format is used. Standardized.

- **Test of Adolescent Language (TOAL)** - Appropriate for adolescents aged 11.0-18.5 years; series of tests measure vocabulary and grammar features of spoken and written language, in both receptive and expressive modes. Composite scores are derived in listening, speaking, reading, writing, spoken language, written language, vocabulary, grammar, receptive language, expressive language. Standardized.

- **Woodcock-Johnson Psychoeducational Battery** - Appropriate for ages preschool through adulthood; a battery of tests that measure cognitive abilities, scholastic aptitudes, academic achievement, and interest in scholastic and nonscholastic activities. Cognitive battery yields scores in verbal ability, reasoning, perceptual speed, memory, reading aptitude, math aptitude, written language aptitude, and knowledge aptitude. Achievement clusters include reading: letter-word identification, word attack (reading nonsense words), passage comprehension (cloze procedure); math: calculation, applied problems; written language: dictation (letters, single words, punctuation marks), proofing (recognizing errors in spelling, usage, capitalization, punctuation); knowledge: science, social studies, humanities (oral questions in each area). Standardized.

- **Wide Range Achievement Test (WRAT)** - Appropriate for ages five years through adulthood; broad sampling of skills in reading (letter and word recognition only), spelling (copying marks, writing name, dictation of single words), and arithmetic (counting, reading number symbols, solving oral problems, written computation). Standardized.

II. Oral Language

- **Test of Language Development** - Primary (TOLD-P) - Appropriate for children aged 4.0-8.11 years; measures oral language skills at the receptive (picture vocabulary, grammatic understanding, word discrimination) and expressive (oral vocabulary, sentence imitation, grammatic completion, word articulation) levels. The following composite scores may be derived: syntax, semantics, speaking, listening, and overall spoken language. Standardized.

- **Test of Language Development** - Intermediate (TOLD-I) - Appropriate for children aged 8.6-12.11 years; measures oral language skills at the receptive (characteristics, grammatic comprehension), and expressive (generals, sentence combining, word ordering) levels. Composite scores may be derived in syntax, semantics, speaking, listening, and total spoken language. Standardized.

III. Listening Comprehension

- **Boehm Test of Basic Concepts** - Appropriate for preschool and kindergarten children; measures concepts which deal with space, quantity, time, and other miscellaneous items. Standardized.

- **Peabody Picture Vocabulary Test (PPVT)** - Appropriate for individuals between 2.6-18 years of age; measures receptive vocabulary skills. After listening to a word, the child must point to the correct picture. Standardized.

- **Stanford Achievement Tests: Listening** - Levels appropriate for mid-first through ninth grades; measures listening skills both in terms of retention of specific details and the organization or understanding of the material as a whole. Child listens to brief passages and then answers multiple choice questions. Standardized.

IV. Reading

- **Durrell Analysis of Reading Difficulty** - Appropriate for students in first through sixth grades; covers a wide range of reading related skills including oral reading, speed, and comprehension; silent reading comprehension; listening comprehension; word recognition/ word analysis; listening vocabulary, sounds in isolation; spelling; phonic spelling of words; visual memory of words; identifying sounds in words; phonics ability. Standardized.

- **Gray Oral Reading Tests** - Appropriate for first through twelfth grades; measures the speed and accuracy of oral reading. Criterion referenced.

- **Test of Early Reading Ability (TERA)** - Appropriate for children aged 4.0-7.11 years old; measures construction of meaning: print awareness in situational contexts (child is asked to read familiar signs, logos, etc.), relational vocabulary (child must select two words that go with a given word), discourse (child retells a story or completes a cloze task); knowledge of the alphabet: letter naming, oral reading of individual words and sentences, proofreading for errors in sentences; conventions of written language; punctuation; left-right orientation, etc. Standardized.

- **Test of Reading Comprehension (TORC)** - Appropriate for grades 2 through 12; measures general vocabulary (child reads three words, e.g., yellow, red, blue, and then must determine which two words from a set of other possibilities are related to the three words);

syntactic similarities (child selects which two of five sentences are most nearly the same in meaning); paragraph reading (child reads a brief passage and then answers multiple choice questions about the passage); content area vocabularies (mathematics, social studies and science): specific vocabulary is measured as in the general vocabulary subtest; reading the directions of school-work (child reads each item and carries out the direction); sentence sequencing (child reads five randomly ordered sentences and places them in a logical, meaningful order). Standardized.

- **Woodcock Reading Mastery Test** - Appropriate for children in grades kindergarten through 12; measures letter identification: naming manuscript and cursive letters; word identification: reading/pronouncing words in isolation; word attack: reading nonsense words; word comprehension; passage comprehension: cloze procedure. Standardized.

V. Written Language

- **Diagnostic Spelling Potential Test** - Appropriate for ages seven through adulthood; measures present level of spelling through dictation of individual words; errors are categorized as phonetic or nonphonetic; also differentiates those students who utilize visual memory strategies and those who apply rules of generalization. Standardized.

- **Spellmaster** - Appropriate for children in grades 1 through 12 (remedial); measures spelling through the dictation of regular words, irregular words and homonyms; specifically and comprehensively identifies those phonic and structural generalizations the child has or has not mastered. Is an effective tool for identifying IEP objectives. Criterion-referenced.

- **Test of Written Language (TOWL)** - Appropriate for ages 7 through 18; student is asked to study a series of pictures and then write a story; the story is evaluated for the level of vocabulary, thematic maturity, and handwriting. Subtests also measure spelling through dictation, word usage (e.g., ability to form tenses, plurals, etc.) and style (e.g., punctuation and capitalization). Standardized.

VI. Math

- **KeyMath Diagnostic Arithmetic Test** - Appropriate for kindergarten through sixth grade; measures the following skills: content (numeration, fractions, geometry and symbols); operations (addition, subtraction, multiplication, division, mental computation, numerical reasoning); applications (word problems, missing elements, money, measurement, time). Standardized.

- **Stanford Diagnostic Math Test (brown level)** - Appropriate for mid-fifth through eighth grades; measures the following areas: number system and numeration (identifying numerals, comparing sets to samples of competence in fractions, etc.); computation (primary facts and skills in solving addition, subtraction, multiplication, and division problems); applications (solving story problems, reading tables and graphs, etc.). Standardized.

- **Test of Early Mathematics Ability (TEMA)** - Appropriate for ages 4.0 through 8.11 years old; measures both informal (acquired through daily living) and formal (acquired through school) mathematics. The informal mathematics categories include evaluation of concepts of relative magnitude (e.g., which of two numbers is larger), counting, calculation (ranging from adding concrete objects to mental addition and subtraction). The formal category measures knowledge of convention, e.g., skill in reading and writing numbers, number facts, calculation (addition and subtraction), base ten concepts (e.g., place value and money concepts). Standardized.

VII. Sensory Processing

- **Detroit Tests of Learning Aptitude (DTLA)** - Includes two test levels, appropriate for 3 through 17.11 years; a series of subtests which assess cognitive and perceptual skills. Provides scores in the following areas: general intelligence, verbal, nonverbal, conceptual, structural, attention-enhanced, attention-reduced, motor-enhanced, motor-reduced. Standardized.

- **Developmental Test of Visual Motor Integration (VMI)** - Appropriate for ages two through fifteen; measures visual perception and motor coordination by asking the child to copy geometric designs of increasing difficulty. Standardized.

- **G-F-W Auditory Skills Battery** - Appropriate for ages preschool through adulthood; measures auditory discrimination (child hears a word and must select the correct picture from a group of similar sounding words); selective attention (child is asked to point to a picture while background distractions range from no noise, fan-like noise, cafeteria noise and voices); memory: recognition (child hears a series of words and then a word in isolation and must recall whether it was included in the series), memory for content (child hears a series of words, then is shown a series of pictures and must point to the pictures not included in the series of words), memory for sequence (child hears a series of words and then must arrange pictures of these words in the exact sequence); sound-symbol: mimicry (child repeats words), recognition (child hears a word presented sound by sound and then points to the correct picture), analysis (child hears a nonsense word and must isolate the first, last or middle sound), blending (child hears a word sound by sound and must then pronounce the word), association (child is shown a symbol and then told a nonsense name for that symbol; on subsequent items of the test, the child must identify the symbol by name); reading (child reads nonsense words), spelling (child spells nonsense words). Standardized.

- **Illinois Test of Psycholinguistic Abilities (ITPA)** - Appropriate for ages 2.4 through 10.3; measures the following skills: auditory reception, visual reception, auditory association, visual association, verbal expression, manual expression, grammatical closure, visual closure, auditory sequential memory, visual sequential memory, auditory closure, sound blending. Standardized.

- **Jordan Left-Right Reversal Test** - Appropriate for ages 5 through 12; measures visual reversals of letters, numbers and words (child proofreads written work and identifies any reversals). Standardized.

- **Motor Free Visual Perception Test (MVPT)** - Appropriate for ages 4 through 8 years; measures visual discrimination, figure-ground, closure, memory, and spatial relations. In all items, the child matches a given item with one of four choices; no motor response is required. Standardized.

- **Prereading Screening Procedures** - Appropriate for kindergarteners and first graders who have not yet been introduced to reading; measures visual discrimination of letter forms (child matches identical letters); visual discrimination of word forms (child matches identical words); visual-visual perceptual motor (child is shown a symbol or word and then asked to select the same item from a choice of four); visual-motor copying (child copies symbols, letters, numbers); visual-motor memory (child is shown symbol and then asked to draw it from memory); auditory discrimination (child hears a pair of words and says whether they are the same or different); letter knowledge (child selects from four choices the letter named). Two supplementary tests include the echolalia test (child repeats a series of words heard); reproducing a story (child retells a story which tester has told him). Criterion-referenced.

- **Slingerland Screening Tests for Identifying Children with Specific Language Disabilities** - Appropriate for children in grades one through six; measures copying of words and sentences, both far and near point; visual discrimination (child matches identical words); visual perceptual-memory (after being shown letters, numbers or words, the child selects the same item from several choices); visual-perceptual-memory-kinesthetic (similar to visual-perceptual memory, except that the child writes response); auditory recall (after hearing letter names, words or numbers, the child writes the item); auditory sounds (the child writes the letter or letters which represent certain sounds); auditory association (the child matches a letter, number, or word spoken by the tester with the same written item). Supplementary tests include the echolalia test (child repeats words and phrases said by the tester); words in context (child orally supplies a missing word in sentences spoken by the tester); auditory story telling (child retells a story told by the tester). Criterion-referenced.

- **Specific Language Disability Test (Malcomesius)** - Appropriate for 6th through 8th grades; measures skills similar to those evaluated by the **Slingerland Screening Tests** (see description above). Criterion-referenced.

- **Test of Visual Perceptual Skills (TVPS)** - Appropriate for ages 4 through 12 years; measures visual discrimination (child matches identical geometric shapes); visual memory (child is shown a geometric shape which is removed from sight and is then asked to select the same shape from several choices); visual-spatial relationships (child is shown geometric forms which are identical with the exception of one form which is oriented in a different direction; child must identify this shape); visual form constancy (child matches geometric forms which are similar, with the exception of size, color, orientation, etc.); visual sequential memory (similar to visual memory, except that a series of forms is presented which must be recalled in the same order); visual figure ground (child is shown a form in isolation and then must find an identical form embedded in the context of other designs); visual closure (child is shown a form and must then select an identical form from a series of incomplete forms). This test does not require any motor response. Standardized.

[1]Glossary of Educational Tests was compiled by Linda Williams, Step-by-Step, Chester, Virginia, 1983.

Selected References

After high school: College. (1985). *Lead*, October, 1985, p. 1.

A Joey success story. (1978). *SLD Gazette*, September, 1978. Newton, MA: Massachusetts Association for Children with Learning Disabilities.

American Psychiatric Association. (1987). *Diagnostic and statistical manual of mental disorders - Revised*. Washington, DC: Author.

Association for Children and Adults with Learning Disabilities. (1988). *ACLD Booklist*. Pittsburgh, PA: Author.

Beyler, A. (1988). The house across the street. *Their World*. New York: Foundation for Children with Learning Disabilities, p. 8.

Blalock, J. W. and Johnson, D. J. (1987). *Adults with learning disabilities*. New York: Harcourt Brace Jovanovich.

Bright, G. and Trusdell, M. L. *Characteristics of learning disabilities*. Paper developed for the Learning Disabilities Council, Richmond, VA.

Brutten, M., Richardson, S. O. and Mangel, C. (1973). *Something's wrong with my child*. New York: Harcourt Brace Jovanovich.

Bryan, T. and Bryan, J. (1978). *Understanding learning disabilities*, (2nd ed.). Sherman Oaks, CA: Alfred Publishing Company.

Campbell, K. (1988). Learning - A struggle and challenge. *Their World*. New York: Foundation for Children with Learning Disabilities.

Craig, T. (1984). Especially for parents - Don't wait and see! *Their World*. New York: Foundation for Children with Learning Disabilities.

Dietz Meyer, M. (1988). Get ready for college. *Their World*. New York: Foundation for Children with Learning Disabilities, pp, 62-63.

Foundation for Children with Learning Disabilities. (1985). *The FCLD Learning Disabilities Resource Guide*. New York: Author.

Frank, R. (1985). Self-esteem building. *Interact*, April, 1985.

Fried, H. (1979). Plain talk about children with learning disabilities. Washington, D.C.: U.S. Department of Health, Education and Welfare.

Gearheart, W. (1977). *Learning disabilities: Educational strategies*, (2nd ed). St. Louis: C. V. Mosby Company.

Gordon, S. *A survival guide for people who have handicaps*. Syracuse, NY: Institute for Family Research and Education.

Guhsey, M. *Behavior management tips*. A paper developed for Weekday Early Education, Richmond, VA.

Kirk, S. A. and Kirk, W. D. (1971). *Psycholinguistic learning disabilities: Diagnosis and remediation*. Urbana, IL: University of Illinois Press.

Lerner, J. W. (1976). *Children with learning disabilities*. Boston: Houghton Mifflin Co.

Lerner, J. W. (1971). *Learning disabilities: Theories, diagnosis and teaching strategies*. Boston: Houghton-Mifflin.

Lillie, D. and Place, P. (1982). *Partners - A guide to working with schools for parents of children with special instructional needs*. Glenview, IL: Scott, Foresman & Co.

Lipper, B. (1983). The winner. *Richmond Times-Dispatch*, November 16, 1983.

Must there continue to be cases like Jimmy? (1978). *SLD Gazette*, November, 1978. Newton, MA: Massachusetts Association for Children & Adults with Learning Disabilities.

Myers, P. and Hammill, D. (1976). *Methods for learning disorders*, (2nd ed). New York: John Wiley & Sons.

National Information Center for Handicapped Children and Youth. (1977). *Closer Look*, Fall, 1977. Washington, DC: Author.

National Information Center for Handicapped Children and Youth. (1984). *NICHCY News Digest.* Washington, DC: Author.

National Information Center for Handicapped Children and Youth. (1987). Procedural safeguards insuring that handicapped children receive a free appropriate public education. *NICHCY News Digest.* Washington, DC: Author.

Nissenbaum, C. (1985). *The problem of learning disabilities - Dyslexia,* (2nd edition). Chevy Chase, MD: Tri-Services, Inc.

Osman, B. (1987). Learning disabilities: A family affair. *Their World.* New York: Foundation for Children with Learning Disabilities.

Osman, B. (1984). Spotting problems and setting a course. *New York Times Fall Survey,* November 11, 1984, Section 12, p. 46.

Parent Educational Advocacy Training Center. (1987). Handicapped Children's Protection Act of 1986 - The attorney's fees bill. *Parent Center News,* September, 1987. Alexandria, VA: Author.

Pastor, D. (1986). Self-control therapy with learning disabled children. *ACLD Newsbriefs,* January/ February, 1986. Pittsburgh, PA: Association for Children and Adults with Learning Disabilities.

Reynolds, M. (1962). A framework for considering some issues in special education. *Exceptional Children,* March, 1962, p. 368.

Rosenthal, J. H. (1973). *Hazy? Crazy? and/or Lazy?* San Rafael, CA: Academic Therapy Publications.

Rozantes, P. (1981). Hints for a happier home. *The Observer,* February, 1981, p. 7.

Scheiber, B. and Talpen, J. (1985). *Campus access for learning disabled students.* Washington, D.C.: National Information Center for Handicapped Children and Youth.

SLD Gazette. (1977, March). Newton, MA: Massachusetts Association for Children and Adults with Learning Disabilities.

Sternberg, W. Self-esteem and your learning disabled child. *HELP.* Arkansas ACLD Newsletter.

Stevens, S. (1980). *The learning disabled child: Ways that parents can help.* Winston-Salem, NC: John F. Blair Publishers.

U.S. Department of Health, Education and Welfare. (1978). *Plain talk about dealing with an angry child.* Washington, DC: Author.

Valett, R. E. (1967). *The remediation of learning disabilities.* Palo Alto, CA: Fearon Publishers.

Virginia Association for Children and Adults with Learning Disabilities. *I'm not lazy. . .I want to; I'm not dumb. . .I try to; I'm not naughty. . .I need help; Maybe it's a learning disability.* Richmond, VA: Author.

Virginia Department of Education. (1986). *Handbook for parents of handicapped children.* Richmond, VA: Author.

Virginia Department of Education. (1980). *Program guidelines for students with specific learning disabilities in Virginia's public schools.* Richmond, VA: Author.

Virginia Department of Education. (1985). *Regulations and administrative requirements for the operation of special education programs in Virginia, 1985.* Richmond, VA: Author.

Virginia Department of Health Regulatory Boards. *Code of Virginia - Chapter 28 - Behavioral Science Professions.* Richmond, VA: Author.

Vogel, S. (1987). LD students in college need self-knowledge. *Update,* Vol. 1, No. 2. Chevy Chase, MD: Tri-Services, Inc.

Wallace G. (1975). *Characteristics of learning disabilities: A television series.* Richmond, VA: The Learning Disabilities Council.

Westhead, E. (1980). *Postsecondary education for the LD student - A few suggestions.* A paper prepared for the Virginia Association for Children and Adults with Learning Disabilities, Richmond, VA.

White, S. Building social skills and self-esteem: How parents can help. *Minnesota ACLD Newsletter.*

Williams, L. (1983). *Glossary of educational tests.* Step-by-Step, Chester, VA 23831.

Wright, P. *Four steps to ensure a free and appropriate public education for your LD child.* 4104 E. Parham Road, Richmond, VA 23228.

Suggested Changes and Additions to the Parent Guide
(Second Edition, 1991)

Please mail this form to

Learning Disabilities Council
P.O. Box 8451
Richmond, Virginia 23226

I suggest the following changes or additions to **Understanding Learning Disabilities: A Parent Guide and Workbook** (Second Edition, 1991)

_____

_____

_____

_____

_____

_____

_____

_____

_____

_____

_____

_____

_____

_____

_____

Submitted by:

_____
Name (Optional)

_____
Address

_____
                              Zip

Phone (_____) _____